THE
RAINBOW BRIDGE

First Phase
Link with the Soul

by
TWO DISCIPLES

RAINBOW BRIDGE PRODUCTIONS
P.O. Box 929
Danville, CA 94526

THE SUN . . . BLACK . . .
ANTAHKARANA

This formula in TEACHINGS ON
INITIATION in DISCIPLESHIP IN
THE NEW AGE Volume II is the
basis of our cover design. The key-
note as we see it is:

LET THE EARTH BECOME A
SACRED PLANET

DINA II Page 321

"Students would do well . . . to pay more attention to the recognition of THAT in them which 'having pervaded their little universe with a fragment of itself REMAINS."

—ESOTERIC ASTROLOGY
by Alice A. Bailey, p. 618

INDEX

PLATES

"THY KINGDOM COME ON EARTH

AS IT IS IN HEAVEN."

—The Lord's Prayer

Has it not been forgotten that the objective of the Great Teacher was to bring the Kingdom of Heaven to Earth and that, in order to do this, He gave the principles which must govern human relationships in the simple invocation: PEACE ON EARTH, GOODWILL AMONG MEN? And is it not evident that such progress as humanity has made has been in proportion to the implementation of this invocation? This invocation is to become a command as the SWORD of the SPIRITUAL WILL governs mankind when wielded by the hand of the Returning Teacher. Thus will the Aquarian Age become manifest. The time is NOW!

INTRODUCTION

The Rainbow Bridge has many definitions and interpretations, both objective and subjective. It will seem to many only a poetic line dealing with ideas and images of great familiarity. On any path or road a bridge spans something which interrupts its use and the bridge becomes a part of the way.

The Path is an occult term used to signify the evolutionary approach to God. Since our environment, both objective and subjective, is composed of matter plus energy in a spectrum from densest matter to the freest energy, the Path is defined also as a movement in consciousness "upward", that is, from involvement in dense forms to those of greater freedom and beauty.

As consciousness functions first in dense forms, it is implemented by the impressions of the five senses necessarily shielded by their own limitations only to a part of the lowest octave which we call the physical plane.

We are coming to a time when a wider range of perception will become more general. This is called, loosely, clairvoyance, clairaudience, telepathy, psychometry, etc. Even at the beginning of such extended perceptions, man appears quite different. This different appearance is described in a preliminary way in this book, with emphasis on a line of light and energy which appears to extend upward into space and downward into the earth. This thread and its growth, use and value to the individual and his contribution and relationship to the whole is the subject of this book.

The thread is, in our approach, an energy or vibration between states of consciousness. It is called, including additions and growth, the antahkarana or, because of the type and appearance of the energy flow which is distinguishable when it is enlarged to a certain dimension, the Rainbow Bridge.

Its appearance has been indicated pictorially, diagramatically and symbolically in the various Plates in this book. It is the vertical arm of the three crosses of occult recognition and teaching (the Cardinal, Fixed, and Mutable Crosses), and it appears in many tables and diagrams in the books of Alice A. Bailey who was the amenuensis for the Tibetan Master, Dwal Khul, the antahkarana or Rainbow Bridge is implied in countless ways throughout the texts. It is also called the sutratma and the sushumna, the latter referring to the lowest thread or corresponding to the physical nerve and the sutratma corresponding to the completed bridge.

On the visible thread disappearing both above and below as well as within the body, there are organized centers of energy. These centers of activity vary widely in appearance, both between themselves and, in time, there appears in them a great deal of change and growth. This change ultimately produces change in the form to which they are related. On this thread, conducted both from above and below, pass those energies and impulses which produce the changes which we call evolution.

There is an important sequence in such changes as they affect the centers of activity, and this sequence relates to the shifting focus of that undefinable condition we call *consciousness*. As consciousness moves from point to point or level to level from earth upward, man's nature changes even though his form appears to be the same; in reality it becomes more refined in the substance and energy of which it is composed. There comes a time when centers above the physical body are touched, and the man finds himself in a state of being which, although new, seems to be the very essence of his being and somehow strangely and wonderfully the essence of *all* being.

When this happens and his consciousness de-

scends and is closed in by his sense of limitation, he is at a loss to describe what has hap-
pened. But the experience carries with it a deep
necessity to impart to others who seem to be
an extension of himself, a part of truth or reality
which he can never question again. In his at-
tempts to do so, limited not only by the strangeness of his experience but by his capacity to
express himself, he speaks of illumination, cosmic consciousness, satori, samadi, and may in-
vent inhabitants of that state with systems, or-
ders of relationship, religions and philosophies
to further describe what he has experienced
which is not only the essence but also all of its
extensions. Needless to say, all such efforts are
ultimate failures because all descriptions are
limitations to that above and beyond.

Besides the sequential activation of the centers on the thread, the thread itself begins to
expand; strand after strand of living, vibrant
energy clothed in color are added, and, at a
certain apparent size, there appears to clairvoyant vision a steady flow of *rainbow fire* from
beyond vision through man and into the earth.
Within his bodies there is radiation, increasing
in time with attachments and lines of energy
flow making triangles of light. At first there
appears to be no difference in his outer vehicles
or life, but, in time, he becomes something different, and he *does not need to die to experience
Heaven.* Such experience is one of the goals of
all occult teaching and practices.

There is a greater goal than personal experience and the inflowing synthetic Seventh Ray energy of the dawning Aquarian Age has made it possible for "little children" (First Degree Initiates) to link with the Logos and thus serve. The effect on their vehicles in the end will be profound, not only in its radiation into the vehicles but as a conductor of energies to be intelligently used to purify the vehicles and to make possible those activities of the true psychic centers which the Soul undertakes to bring into usefulness as soon as possible.

Many who read this book will recognize the term "centers" (chakras) as used in occult literature and referring to the energy structure as seen by developed etheric vision (the lowest stage of clairvoyance). They will also recognize the term "initiation" as referring to the steps in the progress of "enforced evolution".

In this approach to building the Rainbow Bridge the student is warned to ignore the true centers (on the etheric level) as is also advised in the Tibetan yoga. We also point out that the techniques suggested will only be effective for First Degree Initiates (or those of higher degrees) who have already had certain centers activated by the Initiator, the Christ, and which are latent thereafter until the Great Work is again undertaken. Initiates of the Second Degree will recognize the validity of these instructions and those of the Third Degree will need no instruction, except reminder, for they can make direct contact with the Source. To become a Fourth Degree Initiate is to become one of those "friends of the Christ" in the phrase, "Christ and his Nine Thousand Arhats (or in the feminine, the Tahra.)"

A reference to the antahkaraha given in DISCIPLESHIP IN THE NEW AGE, Volume 2, page 266, will be helpful here: "A line, emerging from the earth and ending in the ocean"—referring to the sutratma which, when the antahkarana is completed, blends all types of consciousness, spirit and matter, into one living whole, the ultimate Reality." Also on page 300 in the same book is the following: "The Masters are seeking to hasten in Their disciples this recognition of that which is imminent, so that they can be the intelligent agents whereby the needed precipitations can be brought about. There is a definite technique for producing this peculiar form of cooperation, but it will not be possible to work with it for another twenty-five years." (Published in 1955)

We quote also from the book, THE RAYS AND THE INITIATIONS, page 337, "The mysteries are revealed, not primarily by the reception of information anent them and their process, carried out within the etheric body of the disciple: These enable him to know that which is hidden; they put him in possession of a mechanism of revelation and make him aware of certain radiatory and magnetic powers or energies within himself which constitute channels of activity and modes whereby he may acquire that which it is the privilege of the initiate to own and use."

Our system is based on the modern exposition of Dwal Khul, the Tibetan Master, as given through his amenuensis, Alice A. Bailey; these books have been and are our textbooks! Our purpose in writing this book and any subsequent releases may be broadly stated by quoting from WHITE MAGIC, pages 55-56: "It should always be borne in mind that the work required is twofold:

1. To teach students how to link the personal lower self with the overshadowing soul so that in the physical brain there is an assured consciousness as to the reality of that divine fact. This knowledge renders the hitherto assumed reality of the three worlds futile to attract and hold, and is the first step, out of the fourth, into the fifth kingdom.

2. To give such practical instruction as will enable the aspirant to

   a. Understand his own nature. This involves some knowledge of the teaching of the past as to the constitution of man and an appreciation of the interpretations of modern Eastern and Western investigators.

   b. Control of the forces of his own nature and learn something of the forces with which he is surrounded.

c. Enable him so to unfold his latent powers that he can deal with his own specific problems, stand on his own feet, handle his own life, solve his own difficulties and become so strong and poised in spirit that he forces recognition of his fitness as a white magician, and as one of that band of consecrated disciples whom we call the 'Hierarchy of our planet'."

More specifically, the first point above is our main purpose: "To teach students how to link the personal lower self with the overshadowing soul." This is the first step in building the bridge which will ultimately link all parts of the present, divided, separated man into a unity in his higher principles. This unity within himself shows him very soon that there is an inner unity with other selves, a true brotherhood, and the meaning of service begins to be revealed to him and is automatically expressed outwardly in that "goodwill among men" which the Christ invoked.

The Tibetan Master, Dwal Khul, in his book DISCIPLESHIP IN THE NEW AGE, Volume 2, has given an outer form of the techniques required, but it appears that there is always the need in occult teaching for one who has accomplished the proposed step forward to vitalize the teaching and assist in those difficult first steps, difficulties inherent in the very structure of the lower personal self. It is part of our fundamental purpose to find those who will respond and give such assistance.

Our purpose is much more than personal assistance however. *There is a desperate need at this time for disciples who make this first link, for it enables them as incarnated disciples to ground and, under later instructions, to blend energies needed by the Christ and His Masters for the coming externalization of the Planetary Hierarchy.* Such aspiring students can be of vital use to the Hierarchy from the very start of their work and the simple techniques which have been thoroughly tested and tried. Such work these students are able to do will enable them to take part in this final battle of the Changeover (as the Brothers of Light call it) from the Piscean to the Aquarian Age. The energies which can be invoked and evoked and transmitted into the etheric network of the planet will enable the Christ and his disciples to *shorten* the days of suffering which threaten to overwhelm the planet. *The time is now.* An essential difference between the Piscean and the Aquarian Age is the objective of religious and philosophical thought and its impact on the unthinking masses of humanity.

The Piscean Age emphasized Heaven as an objective above and beyond the life of earth. Consequently, disciples sought by all possible means to reach and enter into that ideal state which they called the Kingdom of Heaven. In it the return of the Christ was a remote objective only to occur when earth itself came to an end. The human body was a sinful obstacle to be ignored or punished, and all that pleased it was the work of the Devil. There was no real or tangible sense of what the return of the Christ really meant.

The Aquarian Age has a different objective. Earth itself must be changed and moved forward in its evolution so that a more suitable environment and opportunity can be provided for the evolution of the kingdoms evolving on earth. This change must be made by humanity, a humanity inspired and led by the Christ and His Church (His disciples who have recognized and worked with Him). The Christ has never left the earth as He stated so long ago. Many have reached Him in the intervening years, but not enough of humanity has done so to complete the preparation for the Aquarian Age. This is no longer the case as the coming decades will demonstrate.

This book will be presented in a limited edition at first and directed to selected persons. We have the means to control the distribution to a large extent. Our choice and its reasons will be clarified as you read and study and, above all, *do something about it.*

This book is a part of a larger book concerning successful techniques developed by *communicators* to form an integrated and successful group called by the White Brothers a Prototype Group. It is limited to the first phase of the work of this group and is intended to be highly selective. It is written in response to the following:

1. Successful work done and approved.

2. A desperate need for more people to·develop the first strand of "The Rainbow Bridge" (the antahkarana).

3. A suggestion by the White Brothers that such a book be written as soon as possible.

4. This book is a forerunner to the teaching soon to be given by Hierarchy as promised by the Christ.

5. It is a part of the Externalization of the Hierarchy.

6. The need of the young disciples destined to make the Changeover is pressing. Many are ready for this teaching now and many thousands are being born or are growing up now; they will need teaching and teachers.

7. And, of course, the world crisis, which appears to have no real leaders with solutions, demands such instruction. The "Children of the Dawn" will *have* solutions, and they are the beginnings of the Auroran Race that will succeed the present Aryan Race.

Recently we were told: "If students will use the Soul Mantram, build the Central Channel, and become anchor points for Hierarchy and transmitters of these vital energies they will serve to externalize Hierarchy and to speed the process. . ." In DISCIPLESHIP IN THE NEW AGE, me 2, page 13, Dwal Khul said: "The times are serious and the world disciples are hard pressed. The Hierarchy and its affiliated groups are seeking active help and cooperation in the work of salvage. All disciples and aspirants are needed, and all can give much if the desire, the loving heart and the consecrated mind are united in service."

The foreword of the book, COSMIC FIRE by Alice A. Bailey, ends with a quotation from the Buddha as given in Volume 3, page 401 of the SECRET DOCTRINE by H. P. Blavatsky. The Lord Buddha has said: . . . that we must not believe in a thing said merely because it is said; nor traditions because they have been handed down from antiquity; nor rumors, as such; nor writings by sages, because sages wrote them; nor fancies that we may suspect to have been inspired in us by a Deva (that is, in presumed spiritual inspiration); nor from inferences drawn from some haphazard assumption we may have made; nor because of what seems an analogical necessity; nor on the mere authority of our teachers or masters. But we are to believe when the writing, doctrine, or saying is corroborated by our own reason and consciousness. 'For this,' says He in concluding, 'I taught you not to believe merely because you have heard, but when you believed of your consciousness, then to act accordingly and abundantly.'"

Since the key to this statement is in the words "of your consciousness" it should be evident that the Buddha did not mean the consciousness of the objective mind but rather the creative energy of the higher or abstract mind or in the light of the Soul which is a growing possibility among aspirants and disciples (witness Bucke's COSMIC CONSCIOUSNESS for examples of this). The intuition is involved here and may appear as a certainty, a pure conviction which is evidence of the energy of that realm called "pure reason", which, like a vast computer, retrieves from the infinite data banks of world memory on all planes.

The same teacher who is responsible for COSMIC FIRE also said that intelligent skepticism has been a protection to modern students and prevented their involvement in fantasy, superstition, misused and misquoted fragments of older teachings and occult charlatans and fakers generally.

Times are changing, and, because the rational mind has no solution for world and individual problems, students and seekers are turning to the subjective worlds—the subjective source of all that is tangible and objective. There are, unfortunately, very few teachers equipped to lead the inquirer safely through the incredible mass of current so-called occult literature and expose the number of false prophets.

So the goal for all students is to approach occult study with an open mind, ready to accept that which is good and reject the false, invoking their own Soul—"In the Wisdom of the Soul, I desire the Truth!"—and confidently expecting that illumination which is the result of contact with the higher mind. When this contact is made, it will not be forgotten, and the student will find *within himself- the touchstone of Truth. This is also our goal for students. Let the day come when you will stand on your own feet, recognize your own duty and responsibility and ask no one to make decisions for you, here, hereafter, inner or outer. Collectively students will help to build the World Antahkarana as they grow individually, and this is the larger goal and the mainspring of our emphasis.*

We close this introduction with the Master Morya's beautiful words as to the bridge of which the Central Channel is a manifestation and a beginning. The bridge will be the present theme of all our efforts, and we urge you to build the bridge as the Brothers of Light and the Christ have done. Become a part of the bridge between Heaven and Earth, between the present age and the new, between that which you appear to be and the Shining One which is your Soul. Only thus can Externalization of the Hierarchy and the return of the Christ be possible.

The Rainbow Bridge has been called in the books which form the basis of our teaching The Antahkarana.

HIERARCHY

HOW·TO·TRANSMUTE·THE·MOST·BITTER·INTO
THE·MOST·SWEET·?·NAUGHT·SAVE
HIERARCHY·WILL·TRANSFORM·LIFE·INTO·ITS
HIGHER·CONCIOUSNESS. IT·IS·IMPOSSIBLE
TO·IMAGINE·A·BRIDGE·INTO·THE·INFINITE
BECAUSE·A·BRIDGE·IS·IN·NEED·OF·ABUTMENTS.
BUT·HIERARCHY,AS·THE·ABUTMENTS·OF·THE
BRIDGE,BRINGS·ONE·TO·THE·SHORE·OF·LIGHT.
AND·IMAGINE·THE·ENTIRE·EFFULGENCE
THAT·THE·EYES·BEHOLD! AND·UNDERSTAND
THE·SONG·OF·LIGHT.
LET·US·LABOR·FOR·THE·LIGHT·OF

HIERARCHY

"HIERARCHY"·AGNI YOGA PRESS - 1933

CHAPTER 1
TEACHING, ANCIENT AND MODERN

Humanity has never, in its long history and even in its pre-history, been left without a teacher. The thread of truth has always been available to those who seek. From time to time, age after age, there have appeared Communicators, who again bring to the attention of humanity, the Path to truth and life and growth in spiritual awareness. The ancient statements are as true today as they ever were, but many expansions, adaptations to the need of any given time in man's growth, and many interpretations have been successfully given. It must never be forgotten that many of these statements and interpretations have been given through men, however dedicated and sincere, and because of this, they have varied somewhat in the telling. Nevertheless, the truth is *there* and available to discriminating students.

Communicators appear to direct the aspirations of men; they did so in every past era and are doing so now. Such a Communicator is the Master Dwal Khul, the Tibetan, who as a former teacher known to us as Confucius left the imprint of His thought upon Chinese philosophy which endures to this day. As the great teacher, Aryasanga, he left numerous works in Tibet which have also influenced an entire people.

Today this Master of Wisdom and Compassion has again given humanity through numerous "works" a modern presentation of the ancient truths with deeper interpretation; these works will provide the basis of teaching which will find expression in the anticipated New Age of Aquarius. The Age of Aquarius is now beginning with the world "housecleaning" seen everywhere. The many books Dwal Khul has presented through his amenuensis, Alice A. Bailey, available either in hardback or softback in most bookstores handling occult or metaphysical literature are also available from the Lucis Publishing Company, 113 University Plaza, 11th floor, N.Y., NY 10003.

Personally we, the authors of this brief book, have had a lifetime of experience in relation to the books mentioned above as well as much application and experiment with the suggestions given therein, not only in the outer contact and promotion, but with the inner and foundation work behind the scenes, which is the real function of occult teaching.

There are many statements throughout His books to the effect that techniques cannot be given. Nevertheless, much was given, concealed or scattered in various ways well known to occult teachers. We have for many years been teachers of a closed group experimenting with the application of hints given in these books and later from Brothers in His ashram. Our group has succeeded in that inner integration which concerns the "higher principles" and which seem so remote and inaccessible to most students.

Since, as has been accepted by science, *all is energy* or matter may be converted to energy as energy to matter, the Ancient Wisdom is presented by Dwal Khul as "The Science of Applied Energy", dealing with the mental concepts and processes through which man's evolution may be "enforced". As the "Science of Purification" He deals with the processes of the emotional nature and the hindering accumulations of mistaken or outworn creations, thought-forms vitalized by desire in man's astral nature. Under the heading "The Science of Redemption" He deals with the release of energy-matter from the accumulation of past creations on all personality levels. This is the way the personal self provides the redeemed matter which the Soul uses to build "The Body of Light." Our closed group has successfully demonstrated, as far as has been individually possible, the existence and application of the three sciences described briefly above and in the book called *THE EXTERNALIZATION OF THE HIERARCHY* on page 693.

In a more personal sense we, and the group we work with, have followed the injunctions given in *EXTERNALIZATION OF THE HIE-RARCHY* beginning on page 692 as follows:

1. "The stage wherein the tainted area, the hidden evil, or the diseased factors are recognized and duly contacted in order to ascertain the extent of the purificatory measures required.

2. The process of discovering the magnetic areas, magnetized in past centuries, and even aeons, by Members of the Hierarchy . . .

3. The stage wherein the disciple withdraws his attention from the source of difficulty and concentrates upon certain mantric us-ages and certain Hierarchical formulas, thus setting loose the energies needed to destroy the germs of evil, latent or active, thus eliminating certain materialistic ten-dencies, and strengthening the soul of all that is to be purified and the life to be found within every form . . .

4. The stage of withdrawing of the purifying energies; this is to be followed by a period of stabilising the purified form and starting the life and soul within it on a new cycle of spiritual growth."

These injunctions have personal, group and planetary significance and application.

In our experience of working with the books written as Dwal Khul has said primarily for First and Second Degree Initiates (Initiates of the threshold and not for the many intellectuals who have not yet evolved to the point of these initiate degrees), we have found it difficult to get such disciples to read and study. Many students who have tried to read such books have said they do not understand them. Such difficulties to understanding will lose their force in the near future because they are due to:

1. The flood of low grade communication in all fields of human interest which causes shallow concentration.

2. The lack of what beginners recognize as specific techniques for the application of occult teachings.

3. The scattering of information relating to a particular subject throughout many books and the use of occult blinds and symbols which appear to be evasions of proper explanation.

4. The basic fact that such books cannot be read and used as text books in the modern scholastic pattern.

How then should they be read?

1. With a persistent, underlying effort to recognize the idea back of the words

which, according to occult definition, constitute ideals.

2. This involves an effort toward telepathic
   reception, since these are *living* books
   through which the writer can be contacted.
   A sentence is often only a key to open a
   door to understanding, a contact with the
   greater thought-form involved. Thus students have often found that one sentence
   held in brooding consciousness (which is
   a real meditation) will hold the attention
   for many hours, sometimes for days.

3. In a book such as WHITE MAGIC, no student will get depth of understanding from
   one straight reading. The book must be
   scanned with the reader paying attention to
   what appeals to him or applies to his own
   life and experience and the rest set aside
   for future understanding.

We have said that all we teach is in what Dwal
Khul has written and that it is usually said better
than we can say it. However, we are trying to
fill a gap, not so much in teaching *about* the
subject as in calling attention to beginning
techniques by the use of which the student-
disciple can make necessary changes in his vehicles.

In the book, DISCIPLESHIP IN THE NEW
AGE, VOLUME 2, Dwal Khul gives all that is
needed as to meditation. According to ancient
practices, however, intermediate incarnated
teachers are needed, i.e., to take a step forward

the helping-hand of one who has already taken that step is required. This indicates that, in the interest of efficiency and communication, such assisting teachers must not be too far ahead of their students in the chain of Hierarchy.

With this all in mind and because the Brothers who are concerned with the observation and assistance of the many newly formed and forming groups have told us it is time to release selectively the First Phase of this teaching, we have decided to offer this book, knowing that this teaching has been successful with the students in our experimental, closed group which has worked steadily for more than ten years.

It may be helpful to many students if some explanation of the creative process by which the Hierarchy inaugurates new teaching, in this case the teaching for the New Age, is given. There is much speculation on this matter, and many claims are made purporting to be the fountainhead of the New Age, but the keys to understanding when and how such teaching is given are quite definite in the Tibetan's books.

First as to the time factor: The principle contributions to the teaching are made at fifty year intervals, i.e., 1875, 1925, and, as has been stated, 1975. Since on the mental and higher planes, *time as we know it* does not exist, we must consider these points in time as being cyclic repetition on the mental plane. Since, on that plane, it is not a simple cycle like a sine wave but a composite, we cannot always interpret on the physical level that the emerging teaching will climax exactly at the dates given. So, in truth, the teaching of the New Age began a long time ago, as we, bound to the *past, present and future* concepts of the physical world, must consider.

In 1875, through H. P. Blavatsky, the Tibetan Master, acting as the "front man" for the Hierarchy, as He called Himself, and more directly for the three Masters who will hold office when the New Age is in full bloom (Morya, Koot Humi, Rakoczi) gave the world THE SECRET DOCTRINE.

In 1925 as the Tibetan Master had prophecied, He gave through Alice A. Bailey the psychological key to understand the SECRET DOCTRINE. Along with this, He also outlined certain other keys which will be "turned" at the cyclic points mentioned (the astrological key, for instance). The revelations of the psychological key were spread over thirty years. Those who study cycles recognize that the energies released are not a single explosion but a gradually increasing tempo which climaxes and then decreases. We are *now* in the increasing phase of the 1975 cycle, and we should take note of world events confirming this fact.

New Age teachings will be *Group Teachings,* and The New Group of World Servers their instrument of implementation. This group possesses sensitivity to spiritual impression and a definite recognition of responsibility to serve.

They will serve in every area of human activity, expressive of the seven ray energies.

CHAPTER 2
EVOLUTION

Evolution is a fact in nature; its ultimate objective is not known. It appears to result in forms of ever greater complexity and capacity to survive, assert themselves, reproduce, relate to others in cooperative effort and to deal harmoniously with and control their environment. These five instinctual activities are all observable and much is known about them in form, activity and history.

A by-product of such actions and capacities appears in what we call subjective ways, i.e., emotion, thought, and self-identification. These also are basically products of evolution as are the other more remote and inaccessible concepts of Soul and Spirit. These realities are also evolutionary and produced in the past. This thought conflicts with the sharply entrenched and dogmatic ideas about creation and origin which still exist.

The times demand new understanding of ourselves to make survival possible. Evolved forms, cultures and civilizations can disappear as observable history shows, and our cultures are not immune. If the suggestions of a cold, scientific universe evolved from units of attraction and repulsion is objectionable, we can only say that if all we call good, beautiful, orderly and progressive is also a product of such simple beginnings, why should we prefer a fairy story? Let us clear away the ragged garments of superstition and face a few facts, among them the basic one of self-determination. That is, we can become what we wish by virtue of and use of evolved capacities to will and to create. Is it not possible that in the unknown worlds of Soul and Spirit toward which we yearn, the ultimate becoming must lead to and through what we call Gods? Something like ourselves evolved infinitely far beyond our present concepts? We say it is so!

Let us therefore evolve together, for the togetherness of groups and grouping appears to be an evolutionary objective. By this approach we propose to relate occult teaching to scientific fact and procedure which tentatively accepts and experiments with hypotheses which appear possible if not yet generally proved.

The urge to betterment is inherent in the driving force of evolution on all levels of development. In as much as this book deals with the power of intangibles such as will, visualization, imagination and thought, let the reader consider the power of this intangible urge to betterment which is neither thought nor imagination but that which drives him into action. The process by which this urge works begins with the *will* which is closest to its nature, continues with the inner formation of a picture of the desired objective, and which is implemented by thought, a technique to accomplish it, and which finally is objectified by action and appearance.

Expressed in individuals this urge varies widely, being modified and directed by the differing capacity for will, visualization, imagination and thought. It is thus possible for it to be misdirected in such a manner as apparently to reverse its intent of betterment. Such failures add to the thought content as meaning of experience and modify the next action forcibly under the Law of Cause and Effect. Thus we progress.

Obviously, the preceeding precepts could be expanded by way of illustration and example, but the emphasis intended here is on *method or technique,* and if the reader follows the injunction "let the reader consider", he will be satisfied by his own applications. The technique is "do-it-yourself" all the way through.

To summarize:

1. Recognize the urge to betterment in your-

self.

2. Identify the particular desire which causes you to read this book. Identify the personal will which is the manifest power of the urge.

3. Think about it *continually.*

4. Prepare to take action with all the force of your will, visualization, imagination and thought which will lead to ultimate success in the evolution of the subjective side of your nature.

INITIATION IS ENFORCED EVOLUTION

The injunction in the above summary to use the force of will is implied or directed in the whole subject of initiating progress.

Dwal Khul has said that Initiation is an abnormal procedure and in many places it is described as "forced" or "enforced". If this is so, what or who enforces evolution? And what is evolution anyway?

Evolution is progressive adaptation to environment and it is also a movement of consciousness upward in the scale of being. It is the response to the will of the Logos, of God. It is the Purpose behind the Plan. It is the movement from multiplicity toward unity. It is God's drawing of all His creation back to Himself.

In His vast cosmos there are many methods,

processes and forms of evolution. We are concerned with one of them. Twenty-one million years ago, inconceivably long ago to our short lives, a successful experiment was completed in an earlier cycle on the planet Venus. A portion of the humanity of that cycle, having submitted and cooperated in a *forcing process,* attained a degree far beyond what was considered normal for that planetary cycle. They had gained all that was to be gained and were masters of all that planet could offer. Their perception was becoming cosmic, and they began to participate in the larger purpose and activity of the Solar System. They considered the planet Earth which was, in a solar sense, a backward planet; its evolutions had not gone beyond the animal stage, and Logoic purpose required stimulation of animal man.

A group of forty-nine Venusians volunteered to assist in the application of the *forcing process* to Earth, and a vanguard crossed space to this planet in physical form; the Hierarchy was founded here on Earth by these forty-nine pioneers. Time meant little to Their exalted state, and they observed. This planet was strange to them in many ways and was not their sole interest which lay in values and activities far beyond our conception. Earth's strangeness was the fact that the life focus of it was developing in a much denser medium than in the Venus cycle, a medium quite resistant to higher energies.

Eighteen million years ago another step was

taken, and a great number of Venus angels (the completed humanity of the Venusian cycle came to earth, not in the more physical vehicles of the first small group, but in bodies which functioned only on our buddhic and atmic planes with lowest anchorage in what we call the higher mind in its seventh aspect. These were the Solar Angels, the Lords of Venus, the Angels of the Presence of the Ancient Wisdom teaching.

Now, all the lives of a planet are linked with the Logos of a planet by threads of what appears to be light but which, like all forms, are matter plus energy or life. The individual forms of the highest animal came and went in the savage battle for survival, but the life at the death of the form projected itself again and again endlessly into the forms whose structure was perpetuated by the genes of the surviving units.

The Angels of the Presence attached themselves to individual threads by another thread which we call the thread of consciousness and "put down a portion of Themselves" which we call the Soul Star. They "remained" in their own environment and paid little attention to their attached animals, now self-conscious, individualized, because of the consciousness thread and potential Souls through the Soul Star. The Angels stimulated the growth of the brain and our archaeologists wonder why the big brain appeared with latent capacities in advance of the needs of survival. With the Hierarchy of which They were a part, They controlled environment and made it possible for humanity en masse to survive.

For us, Earth's humanity, the "I" of self, is a fragmented and thus limited part of a Solar Angel. The nature of this limitation varies widely as did the Souls Themselves. Seven great groups they formed, and these are defined in what the wisdom teaching calls the Soul Ray. Their purpose with us will not be accomplished until we become "Soul-infused Personalities", until we become something like what the Initiate Jesus demonstrated two thousand years ago.

Hitherto, those humans who attained made a contribution in some creative field of human activity and withdrew, continuing their work as members of the Planetary Hierarchy or selecting one of the six paths which lead away from the Planet Earth into some area of cosmic service. In what is called the Program of Externalization *now going on,* many will reincarnate to prevent what would be a catastrophic ending of a planetary cycle. It is most difficult for the first of this vanguard, for the environment is unsuited to them and proper parents are usually unavailable. But, humanity is responding and, in the end, Christ and His Church or the Planetary Hierarchy will appear openly among us.

This has been written to emphasize what has been so often said and so little comprehended: "The Soul does the work." "Let the Warrior within fight your battles."

The personality aspires, cooperates, invokes, prays, yields, controls its animal self. When this attitude and action prevails, the Soul turns its attention and effort decisively downward and proceeds with a positive *scientific process* to change, transmute, and take over the vehicles of the personality as the culmination of its own long effort and intent.

If this process had not begun in you, you would not be interested in the wisdom teaching. You are on the Path and are fringe members of the Planetary Hierarchy. Your progress will be according to the measure of Soul-infusion and your cooperation with Hierarchical intent, the Plan.

The Soul does the work. Look to the Soul; yield to the Soul. Let this concept and intent be beneath all your action and thought, a "brooding consciousness", which will take you into the Light, solve your problems, transmute your bodies, and lift you into that next stage of evolution, The Kingdom of Heaven.

CHAPTER 3
WORLD SERVERS

An excellent description of the New Group of World Servers may be found in **WHITE MAGIC** on pages 604-608.

All members of our inner and outer group are members of the New Group of World Servers, either conscious or unconscious. Even if unconscious of status and not working directly and intelligently at some world problem, all the group are transmitters of energy, the quality of which and the direction of which is conditioned by individual development. This and the attitude toward the environment causes students to be a force for those changes which will bring in the New Age. If students work conscientiously and consciously, they become a *power.* This is the hope and the intention embodied in our teaching and contacts.

At this particular time in world history the major work and focus of the Hierarchy (Men who have evolved beyond humanity) is on the problems of humanity and the solution of those problems. Hierarchy is occupied with the seven major areas of human action and expression and are seeking to bring about new orientation and attitudes in humanity. Since all energy comes from the One Source, *all energy is Spiritual,* and the seven areas of human action provide the avenues of expression for spiritual energy (The Seven Rays). The seven areas of action are:

Ray 1 — WILL or POWER
Symbol: The Sword or Baton

Government and Politics; International Relations; Executive Action.

Ray 2 — LOVE-WISDOM
Symbol: The Crossed Pens

Education and Teaching; Communication—using the "media": writing, speaking, radio, television, and audio-visual methods.

Ray 3 — INTELLIGENT ACTIVITY
Symbol: The Spider Web

Finance, Trade, Business; Economics in all its aspects including manipulations. All other human activities (the last four days) on the physical level of life stem from or are related to this Ray because they are Rays of Quality and are specialized types of intelligent activity.

Ray 4 — HARMONY THROUGH CONFLICT
Symbol: The Balance or Scales

Sociology, including race and culture; application of the principles of cooperation and conciliation. Creative aspiration as expressed through all the arts.

Ray 5 — CONCRETE MIND AND SCIENCE
Symbol: The Crucible

The human capacity to think, plan, design, concentrate, reconstruct the world and all else. The Sciences, including medicine and psychology.

Ray 6 — IDEALISM AND DEVOTION
Symbol: The Chalice

Religion and Ideology; Philosophy. All concepts and aspiration for the good and true.

Ray 7 — ORGANIZATION AND RITUAL; MAGIC: EXTERNALIZATION
Symbol: The Crystal; the Torch; the Energy of Life

Structuring of society through Institutions and the ordering of Power through Ceremony, Protocol, and Ritual.

On page 606 in WHITE MAGIC, the telepathic communicators are described. This group is the beginning of the great process called Externalization, for all are members of the White Brotherhood, the Hierarchy. Objective interpretations, usually made, are incomplete and in this sense, wrong, i.e., the assumption that communication is in terms of the "media" used—writing, speaking or audio-visual. While this type of communication is used in the beginning and is necessary because no other method is possible, the *essence* is not contained nor given in long conversation nor dictation by superiors in the evolutionary scale. It means, in one important sense, that the communicator can " go where They are", and there, as One of Them stated, "questions and answers are one." This is the goal for all students—that all may go where They are—for *we truly know only what we experience.*

May you soon recognize that you belong among the group of First Degree disciples and that you have, to some extent, illumined minds as mentioned on page 605 in WHITE MAGIC and that you will eventually, if you work toward it, become first "organized observers" and later "telepathic communicators". The process is embodied in the last stanza of the Disciple's Mantram:

". . .And standing thus revolve,
And tread this way the way of men
And know the way of God"

and this state is the "dual life of the disciple."

There is a spiritual government for this planet; it is called the White Brotherhood, the Planetary Hierarchy, the Society of Illumined Minds, Just Men Made Perfect and by numerous other names. The Christ is the official head of this Brotherhood. He is not the Master Jesus, who was, at the time of his life we know about a Third Degree Initiate. The Masters of the White Brotherhood or Hierarchy are illumined but not the Illuminati which has been publicized as a secret financial and mentalist organization which seeks by all means, fair and foul, to control humanity to its enslavement. They are not the Fabians who are stated to have similar objectives.

The Hierarchy fosters the evolutions of this planet but does not interfere in any personal sense. They offer guidance on occasion through their members such as the Buddha, Jesus, and others. Their present plan is for active participation in all departments of human activity by many incarnated individuals, made possible by the greater development of a large number who have in some past life reached a point of unfoldment where they can become leaders and teachers. The period known as the Renaissance was such a time, but very few were available to become the artists, writers, musicians, philosophers, teachers, etc. who broke the hold of the Dark Ages on mass consciousness in Europe and made our present culture possible.

The apparent dismal and disintegrating condition of human institutions and the many conflicts of today are the result of evolutionary processes. Cyclically, natural law would take effect, and the civilizations and cultures would come to an end and rebuild on a higher turn of the evolutionary spiral taking what we would consider great periods of geologic time. At this time however, the Planetary Hierarchy is intervening to prevent a setback in evolutionary time. This is only possible because many millions of high grade individuals have reached a stage of evolution where incarnation in great numbers to accelerate evolutionary processes is not only possible but is going on rapidly, especially during the last forty years (1930-1970). These are the members of the New Group of World Servers.

At the beginning of this period there were less than five hundred incarnated individuals on the planet who had reached the required stage of evolution. By the year two thousand there will be millions of them, which means, in some areas, a great number of the new born. Many of the youth of today are really different from the mass consciousness of the past, as different as if they really came from another planet in advance of this one!

It has been recognized that the culture and civilization of the time is due to the efforts of very few individuals in all departments of human activity. What then can we expect when a large number of qualified personalities are taking part, taking over, as they will do? The result will be nothing less than the long prayed for New Age, sometimes defined as the Millenium, thus indicating a cycle and a higher state of development.

This changing tide is accelerating rapidly in all nations, cultures, races, and groups, and, when mature, these individuals will change the world and a cycle of a different kind will have its permanent effect, a cultural change beyond present recognition. The Planetary Hierarchy has called this incoming group the New Group of World Servers, and its advent is preliminary to what has been called an Externalization Program in which certain members of the Brotherhood will acknowledge their status and serve openly to guide the incoming Servers. This will be done gradually, and lesser, bridging disciples will come first. A few from among the New Group of World Servers, called Communicators, will be among the very first.

The urge to change is upon the New Group of World Servers, but is undisciplined and violent in many cases. While far in advance of mass humanity, they still have a long way to go to reach the possible evolutionary goal set by Hierarchy. They, therefore, need as much assistance as possible. In general, the parents they have chosen for reasons of past association are not up to their grade, and this has caused much difficulty and pain for all concerned. Some are more fortunate; the greatest good fortune of all, say the old commentators, is in having parents qualified to bear "the Children of the Dawn", a pictorial phrase used by Will Levington Comfort.

Among these incoming workers there are "strong Souls experimenting unwisely" (quoting the Tibetan Master, Dwal Khul), and these, with lesser imitators, are also causing themselves and others much distress and in some cases permanent damage to themselves for this incarnation.

Our objective is not to build an organization nor a cult but to reach a few who are qualified to help others, and to allow them to build as they choose. Their innate impulse to serve will guide them, and there are abundant sources of material to study and apply in the writings of Alice A. Bailey who cooperated with the Tibetan Master, Dwal Khul, as his amenuensis. We constantly and emphatically refer students to these writings.

The growth to be made leaves students free to apply in service what they have gained. This is their responsibility and choice, not ours. The karmic responsibility of occult teaching is quite enough for us and should not be taken lightly by anyone.

The Tibetan Master, Dwal Khul, has given a relationship which is the key to externalization:

This triangle represents that established unity which forms a bridge between Humanity and Hierarchy.

The time has come for the Children of the Dawn to find each other and to work together in the service of the world and humanity. Preparation for this work has been called purification of the three periodic vehicles—mind, emotion and etheric-physical bodies. The processes by which this may be accomplished have been called by Dwal Khul, The Science of Applied Energy related to the mental body, the Science of Purification, relating to the emotional body, and The Science of Redemption, relating to the etheric-physical body. Together, these sciences are called the process of Enforced Evolution or the Path of Group Initiation. To follow the processes of Enforced Evolution or Initiation, purpose, plan, and an understanding of precipitation is required.

The preparatory work serves to eliminate the impurties which are by-products of evolution and which exist in everyone; these impurities are found in each one of the personality vehicles. They are the result of Instinctual Evolution and still exist in the etheric body of the planet and of individual man. They are, in the emotional or astral body, the result of excessive emotional development and extremes of desire, both positive and negative. They are, in the mental body, the result of incomplete mental growth and imperfect thinking.

As one of the agencies through which the Biblical "Little Children" (First Degree Initiates) may be assisted in the preparation for their destined work, we present in this book the First Phase of the techniques of the three sciences named above. The Brother who contacts us when necessary has told us this phase should be written and presented as an aid in the preparatory work of Externalization. Selection of students is to be left to those whose sensitivity, intuition, and sense of responsibility moves them to test the work presented in this book in their own experiences. To aid in the selection of qualified students, we have described their characteristic attitudes under the heading. The Acceptances and Convictions in Chapter 4 and "Qualified People" in Chapter 6 with a suggested screening questionnaire.

CHAPTER 4
THE ACCEPTANCES

To find qualified students who can follow the techniques offered in this book with success, certain acceptances and convictions should be a part of the student's consciousness:

1. There is *One* all inclusive, powerful Principle, Life, Being, Existence, Intelligence, God.

2. There is a Law of Rebirth or Cyclic Return. Reincarnation is a fact.

3. There is a Law of Cause and Effect or Karma.

4. There is a Law of Unification on the Path of Return.
   All Souls are unified in the One Soul of Humanity.

These acceptances underlie all of this work

but do not, as yet, have clear recognition in the brain consciousness of most students. Response to our simplified version of the "secret doctrine" will vary. The more purification and clarity existing in individual students the more quickly will response in the form of understanding come. We expect *all* students to look to the sources of the information we give with more eagerness and response. What we warn against is the smug response that "we know this already". There will be familiar teaching or so it will appear, but what we have to say is linked to **PROCESS** which is distinctly *not familiar* as the condition of the vehicles, the life environment and the field invariably show. From the very beginning, the emphasis in our work has been placed upon processes and *how* to grow spiritually, even to the neglect, somewhat, of the fundamentals "about" occult teaching. For the present, we shall confine ourselves to what THE LIGHT OF THE SOUL calls "spiritual reading", which we have already defined.

ACCEPTANCE NUMBER ONE. It is generally accepted by intelligent people everywhere that there is a guiding principle operative in the universe, no matter by what name it is called or recognized. Order and system and plan in the unfoldment of nature — mineral, vegetable and animal as well as human — is known and accepted by scientists and religionists as well as average people today, at least under the term "natural law". The universe is growing, expanding and developing, and we all *know it*.

This used to be a mere belief, an emotional response, but this is no longer true. Knowing relates to the development of mind which has become universal in this century.

There is one all inclusive, all powerful Principle, Life, Being, Existence, Mind, God. All scientific thought has always sought a simple beginning, a basic unit from which all things are made. This thought has progressed far, but not yet as far as the ancient teaching which says in effect that *space* was the beginning and that units of attraction and repulsion appeared therein and proceeded by their simple qualities plus motion to build all forms and time and space itself as we seem to know them. This is the startling addition: all forms, both objective and subjective—spirit, mind and emotion and all qualities good and bad—are also products of this awesome simplicity.

It is not to be expected that this will be accepted without something like terror (the Tibetan Master says that truth *can be* terrifying). If it is recognized that goodness and beauty and truth came from this oneness of beginning, why should the processes of involution and evolution be terrifying and unacceptable? Is the anthropormorphic God—made in the likeness of man—less horrifying with His balancing counterpart in the form of the Devil, in their unexplained and irrational relationship to the poor clay which they have modelled and with which they play their ghastly games of life and death with Hell and Heaven behind the goal posts?

The disciple does not choose this!

In man, blinded as he may be by the fogs of superstition and belief, there is a common aspiration to something better and higher if only in terms of material living, emotional satisfaction, and mental awakening.

For the disciple for whom this is written, such aspiration is lighted by the conviction and intuition that beneath all manifestation there is plan and purpose, and, though they may not discern the ultimate Being, they are sure that there is love and joy to be found and won on the journey of life to which they are unknowingly committed, and that there is a Kingdom and a Power and a Glory awaiting their conscious awareness and experiencing.

ACCEPTANCE NUMBER TWO. The Law of Rebirth is a concept quite generally accepted by thoughtful men everywhere today. One reason for general acceptance is human recognition of the fact that no one is perfect at the end of any one life and that many opportunities are needed to unfold the perfect, inclusive consciousness planned for mankind. None of us has ever known a human being, however good, who had no weaknesses and no need to deepen his consciousness. And so we have, in the plan, infinite opportunity for experience and the growth into perfect consciousness.

There is a Law of Rebirth or Cyclic Return. Reincarnation is a fact. This the disciple knows as an innate conviction: the form is not the Life, and there is an essence which continues, not perhaps the trivialities of memory which seem to form the personal self. These, recorded in the computer cells of the physical brain, have no future beyond those cells, except as some essence which may be extracted by more subtle forms when the outworn shell with its gossamer web of cells is left behind.

Who remembers, or cares to remember, the infinite detail of yesterday's action? If there is that which binds desire, desire will build anew in another place with another name. The Law is just and accurate, and there is endless time patiently to repeat that which is needed; many shells are left on the shores of Life's boundless sea.

Reincarnation is a fact. Yes! but what incarnates again, the mouldering dust of forgotten graves, the swirls of spent emotion, the shapes of half-formed thought? Not these, the lost, but that which used them, the Shining One (the Soul) enduring in its irridescent palaces, striving downward to awaken in the mind of earth that which will stir and build itself a garment suitable for Gods.

ACCEPTANCE NUMBER THREE. The Law of Cause and Effect is a part of the experience of everyone. If we make a mistake we suffer the consequences or, alternatively, if we perform right action, we enjoy its benefits. This is all that karma and dharma means. But, since we have lived many lives and made many mistakes to reach the point where we now have some good judgment and ability to guide our lives with a degree of wisdom, we know the validity of this law.

There is a Law of Cause and Effect. The very breath attests to this; reaction follows action. All live in and with this Law. The smallest movement, the faintest thought produces causes bringing inevitable effects—the twin existences clasping each other eternally, seeking that union which is barred by time. There is no instantaneous effect; the hardest steel must yield before it moves. Time takes its toll between. The result, the effect, is bound to that which created it, an integral part, inseparable, eternal, bridging if need be from life to life, from eon to eon.

Can this be changed or are we bound on an endless wheel of cause becoming effect and that in turn a cause? Yes, the wheel may be stopped, its structure broken, only by a greater cause. And, when we know the Law, we can make it our servant and thus build that which the Soul intends. The basic Law of Evolution, God's will, is grinding slowly or is changed if we can endure. The debt may be paid in better coin and made to buy that which will serve the desperate need of Earth. This does not deny but affirms a law—a law which if it ceased but for a moment, all things would vanish, for it is the very motion of the *primal* sparks.

ACCEPTANCE NUMBER FOUR. Many

sense the fact that all Souls are part of the one human Soul, but this fact is not yet generally recognized and accepted. This causes certain segments of the human race to feel superior to certain others and to hold unreasonable prejudices. There has been a great deal of talk and thought about brotherhood, but very little practice of the concept as yet. Ultimately, when etheric vision is more generally developed in humanity, men will know their fundamental brotherhood as Souls and act from knowledge rather than from belief.

There is a Law of Unification on the Path of Return. All Souls are unified in the One Soul of Humanity. This is not a becoming; it is the *present truth.* All men are Brothers on the level of Soul. The Path of Return is a path of conscious awakening to a divine fact. Here we are separate, parted by the shells of form which are pierced by the arrows of feeble senses for crippled communication! We can see "as through a glass darkly", a distorted vision. Yet these same senses developed slowly and consecutively by the painful impacts of a brutal evolution of form (or so it seems!) are a promise of the future. The veils grow thin; the higher correspondences are there to be won, and *must* be won! There are many among the young, the Children of the Dawning Age, who glimpse with wonder the light behind form, the swirling glory that waits recognition, the glowing signs of that which waits, the rim of Heaven's World.

The Four Acceptances described in the last

few pages are inherent in disciples. Sometimes, however, they are not so clearly recognized by students who express their ideas in less philosophic and more direct form—in their convictions. Not all persons, no matter how *nice* nor how many years of reading and study are in the background can do the purifying work successfully. Only those, even the very young and unlearned, can do this work who have certain built-in convictions which are the outer evidence of an inner state of consciousness and development. These convictions are usually expressed by the student who is ready to begin this work and, as given here, provide some guidance to those who would like to gather a small group together to do Phase One. These are:

1. A belief in the continuity of life and consciousness.

2. A conviction that there is something in or above which is higher or deeper and worth striving for.

3. A certainty that there is a way to reach this higher consciousness.

4. An acceptance that there is a way involving methods of thought, feeling and action which can change the future and improve the conscious self.

5. An intuitive vision of the fact that there must be those who have found the way and succeeded. Some persons will recognize

the different scale and variation of knowledge of those around them, some knowing a great deal more and some knowing a great deal less than themselves. Some persons will recognize that some have found the way and mastered all to be known through the evolution of man, the Masters. Others will think of these men as members of the White Brotherhood or of the Planetary Hierarchy.

6. A sense of personal responsibility to make the effort in spite of all personal obstacles. This means a willingness to devote time, money, energy, and one-pointed attention or whatever seems likely to speed progress to the goal.

7. A motivation, not only for self-improvement but for service—to be able to serve others with what is gained.

8. In older students, a complete dissatisfaction with methods tried in the past and a readiness for something new and different.

9. Younger students should show these convictions in their attitudes and responses, older students in the events of their lives.

We have, in the past, accepted students and given material only to those whom we could contact personally and verify the indications from the use of a questionnaire and from clairvoyant observation that they could do the work successfully.

Since this may not be possible with many who read this book, we shall try to limit and direct its distribution in other ways. There are individuals for whom contact with our statements may stimulate ancient knowledge and bring them into the "danger zone" so often mentioned by true teachers. This could only come from unwise experiment and from directing attention to the true psychic centers or combining ideas with other techniques and pictures. What we give is amply protected if followed as given.

When and if students become ready for the next phase of clearing, Phase 2, and if they desire to continue, we shall try to anticipate their need and a way to meet it. Time will show the answer to this.

At the time of this printing, the Phase 2 instructions are given in the book "Rainbow Bridge II," available from bookstores or Rainbow Bridge Productions.

CHAPTER 5
THE SCIENCE OF APPLIED ENERGY
Phase One: Building the Central Channel

The beginning technique is designed to test the sincerity, persistence, aspiration, motivation, and initiative of the student. He or she must demonstrate that directions will be followed and that results are achieved through personal and individual effort. The work done is fundamental and the result absolutely essential before any other type of work can be given. The average applicant to this teaching has some radiance about the head and "the spark which hangs from the flame", the tiny soul-star above his head may be no more than a recognizable radiant point of light as seen by clairvoyant vision. He or she also has a noticeable degree of sensitivity and a recognized responsibility to serve mankind as much as he can. It has been found that this soul-star will respond and become more active when the mind is centered upon it. When this occurs, the probationary test period of the individual work may be started. No one can predict the length of time any phase of this work will take because it depends upon individual karma as well as upon application, effort, and persistence of each individual who undertakes it; this is the effort made by the aspiring personality, but this effort alone is not enough. The soul or inner spiritual self must cooperate; if the soul cannot or will not cooperate, nothing can or will be done!

Most people, inwardly, look like walking thunder clouds-dark and turbulent and dangerous and quite unpleasant, except for the few who show radiance in the upper area of the electromagnetic field (the aura) and the bright point of light overhead. (See Plate 1) People are almost entirely obscured by the heavy load they carry around. Sensitive people feel this heavy atmosphere of others around them and generally tend to shun crowds and all but a certain few whom they find tolerable; of course, others feel the same way about them! Just what is this cloudy, unpleasant "mess" around people? A lot of it is the effluvia from their own bodies - dead and discarded material they have not completely eliminated - but also it is a "collection" they have magnetized to themselves and allowed to gather in the electro-magnetic field as they have moved through the activities of daily life. This constitutes the "cloud", the loose churning material that fills the energy structures known as the subtle bodies - etheric or vital, astral or emotional, and the lower mental body or concrete mind.

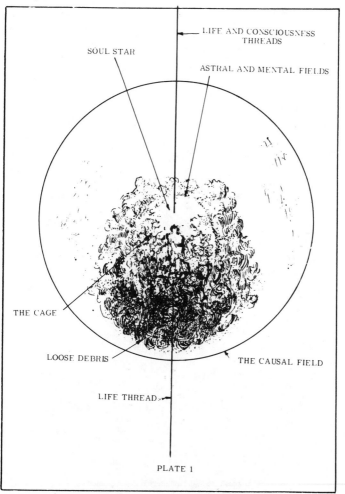

PLATE 1

In addition to the loose material around a person, there is a more permanent and denser structure which may be termed a "cage" because it encloses him entirely and shuts him off from the outside world, distorting every stream of energy sent either to or from him. Without the "cloud" of loose material, this cage appears as a loosely organized series of linked distortions which move with him through every act of his life. (See Plate 2) These appear to be extruded from within, though the seeds for their growth come with the incarnating person;

DENSER MATERIAL ADHERING
TO BODY

SOUL STAR OBSCURED BY
IDEALIZED THOUGHT FORMS

FIELDS CLEARED OF DEBRIS
REVEALING CAGE OF
PLATE 2   RETAINED THOUGHT FORMS

his reactions to his life and experiences cause them to grow and to take form. They are representative of habitual reactions to the events of living.

Close to the body and adhering to it are heavier, more resistant aglomerations of energy-substance which are an extremely individual but of even a more limiting nature. These have been seen by clairvoyants who have thought, quite reasonably, that they were a mark of individuality; they are — *but* they are undesirable residue from the past and must be removed through the processes of purification or clearing. In esoteric terminology, the lower vehicles — physical-etheric, emotional, mental — are all composed of types of the fire produced by friction. The innate, inert and latent force of the physical atoms combined with the electrical force of the etheric or vital body (prana) is built into these resistant hindering forms; the electrical energy-substance of the bewildering, deceiving, illusory emotional nature, conditioned by old controls and ancient habit, is also compressed into this confining layer of material. The figments of a person's own thinking which appear to shine with their own light, false notions, the distorted and outgrown ideals also contribute an obstructing and hindering structure which veils the truth and shuts a person away from direct experience and knowledge of inner reality. (See Plate 2 for forms adhering to the body.)

During the long period of growth and evolution, each human being has built these obstacles to the free expression of his spiritual self. Evolution of consciousness has been an extremely slow and arduous process, largely achieved by trial and error and by discarding old ideas and notions as new and better ones have been found. Much of the "discarded old" still clings to men in one form or another, and it is this that must be eliminated from the vehicles. Roughly, these discards fall into four types in four zones:

1. Those above the head and down as far as the neck which are in the nature of false or outgrown ideals. These are called the idealized thought-forms.

2. Those about the neck and upper back, shoulders and chest which seem to pertain largely to negative ideas and feelings about personal value or worth though, of course, there are some positive patterns of self-evaluation also; these are called the worthless patterns or self-evaluation complexes.

3. Those around the mid-section of the body which seem to be composed of the more destructive ideas and feelings like hate, fear, anger, and extremes of selfishness and self-centeredness. Also here are patterns of helpfulness (which is often interference), possessive love, and those produced by attitudes of sacrifice which make a person into a self-created martyr; these are all the result of misdirected emotion.

These are called the emotional patterns.

4. Those gathered in the lower torso area and about the hips and lower back are related to the instincts which are all rooted in fear- self-preservation, herding, sex, animal curiosity, self-assertion, the sense of possession or territory, the belief that one is separate. These are the instinctual pat- terns.

5. This zone is really an extension of the fourth but appears to be so distinct in most people that we give it special mention. The patterns clustered around the feet repre- sent conditions in life that the person would like to run away from but can't; they inhibit action and motion and are power- fully restrictive.

A great deal more could be said about the res- trictive thought-forms and patterns; the above is merely an indicative description. No abso- lutely hard and fast rule can be applied to these patterns from the past which interlock and in- terlace and link into the body in unusual and unexpected ways.

It is realized that there is practically nothing in occult literature of the past to confirm the specific statements that have been made here. This is undoubtedly due to the fact that those ready for this type of work were so few that they were given special training and attention by trained clairvoyants in monasteries, lamasaries, convents and other retreats apart from **mass** humanity. Times have changed greatly and aspiring students of the ancient wisdom have to learn and receive guidance while living among mass conscious men and in spite of the difficulties this causes. There are many people in the world today who have some clairvoyant faculty but very few who have mastered the many levels of consciousness full development requires. Few clairvoyants admit that they see more than others and there is much conflicting opinion among them; few realize or recognize the differences in people and nearly all refuse to see what is unpleasant to look at. There has been no significant contribution to the descriptions of thought-forms since Charles Leadbeater and Annie Besant published their books early in this century. There was one significant contribution made by Madame Blavatsky in OLD DIARY LEAVES which we have attempted to reproduce with Leadbeater's comments and our own. (See Plate 3)

Plate 3 is a fair copy of Madame Blavatsky's precipitation on silk of the aura of Mr. Stainton Moseyn. Mr. Moseyn was a high-grade disciple who contributed much in the early days of the Theosophical Society. In spite of the quality of the reproduction, there are shown a number of characteristics which our observations have confirmed:

1. The boiling, churning field and some indications of the "cage".

2. The unusually well-developed heart center

located on the surface of the dark background of thought-forms.

3. The presence of solar prana or vital force indicated by scattered points of light.

4. Conventionalized radiations from the heart and head centers.

5. An earth energy, the apas tattva, shown in

small wave-like forms.

This picture appears in OLD DIARY LEAVES, Volume I, page 364 by Colonel Olcott. It provides a typical example of the inner appearance of an advanced disciple, then and *now*.

In THE MASTERS AND THE PATH on page 118, C. W. Leadbeater comments on his illustrations of the astral and mental bodies of men at various stages of their progress as given in his earlier book, MAN, VISIBLE AND IN-VISIBLE: "Those illustrations, however, gave only the exterior appearance of those bodies— that part of each vehicle which is always in relation with the astral or mental world round the man, and is therefore kept in a condition of fairly constant activity. We must remember that these ovoids of astral and mental matter are only superficially vitalized, and that in the case of the average man the surface layer which is thus affected is usually thin. There is always a large proportion in each vehicle which is not yet vivified—a heavy core which takes almost no part in the outer activities of the vehicle, and is indeed but little moved by them. But though this mass of comparatively inert matter is scarcely influenced by the more awakened portion, it is quite capable of acting upon the latter in certain ways. . . . .

"This lethargic mass of unillumined matter has a certain life and tendencies of its own, which assert themselves when the more active part of the personality is somewhat in abeyance, and that happens more especially when the man himself is not actively using those bodies. These qualities naturally vary with different people, but an intense egotism is almost always prominent. The thoughts and impressions generated by this sluggish kernel are often those of conceit and self-glorification, and also of instinctive self-preservation in the presence of any danger, whether real or imaginary . . .There is a long period of slow unfoldment during which this heavy core is being gradually permeated by the light, being warmed and thawed into glowing response."

Students should have no difficulty in relating these quotations to what they are learning about the thought-forms which indeed act along the lines indicated by Mr. Leadbeater. Note that he says the outer layers are activated first. He also says: "In some exalted moment an inrush of power from the ego may temporarily raise the standard of the personality, while on the other hand a steady pressure from the unused portion of the astral or mental body may for the time appreciably lower it."

We have said that, while the thought-forms exist, downpours of energy from the Soul are deflected by them. Mr. Leadbeater either did not exactly identify what he saw or thought it inadvisable to describe it more fully. He does note that these sluggish portions in the aura are a very bad influence. He speaks of the "glowing response" when these negative factors are permeated by the light; we say that the imprisoned

energy is redeemed or liberated. We also call
your attention to the fact that the response of
old thought-forms is often far from "sluggish".
Mr. Leadbeater has said nothing about the
rather specific origin of thought-forms nor
given anything but the vaugest suggestion as to
their elimination.

We have already spoken of the three sciences
named by Dwal Khul as the basis of the new
teachings and therefore begin our techniques
with the mental approach: The Science of Applied Energy.

Every religious movement and spiritual
teacher has emphasized the need for purification, but the purification required has nearly
always been interpreted in physical terms - to
practice celibacy (abstinence from sex), to be
a vegetarian, to fast and pray, to keep the body
clean, to observe certain dietary practices, etc.
etc. These have all been essential guidelines for
humanity in the time when men were victims of
their uncontrolled appetites and instincts, and
these techniques are still useful for people who
are the victims of their instincts and appetites
- who are gluttonous, drunken, self-indulgent
in sexual practice or amoral and promiscuous
or practicing some type of perversion with re-
gard to sex; victims of the instincts also include
those who cannot bear to be alone, who are
pruriently curious, who are excessively possessive, etc. However, purification means a great
deal more than this; it means purifying the
lower bodies or instruments of all obstructions

and hindrances to fusion with the soul and a building process which will lift up and transform the very substance of these instruments so that soul infusion will be possible. This deeper and more fundamental clearing can only be done by the scientific use of energy.

Energy is not a vague, amorphous "something" which we can classify as "spiritual" and then confidently expect it to do the purification with no effort on our part! The scientific use of energy enables us to devote our effort to a process of clearing and to understand what the process is, why it is used, and what it accomplishes as sequential steps are taken. Energy is a synthetic term, as white is a synthetic color. Within the color we call white all other colors of the spectrum are to be found; this fact is easily demonstrated by passing a beam of white light through a prism. Each color in the spectrum represents a frequency, a characteristic vibration, but it is known that this band of color extends in both directions beyond the visible spectrum and that it expresses in related frequency intervals or modulations. The energies we come to recognize and use are of this nature, and, perhaps, could be termed ultra-high frequencies, the spiritual energies. As a start however, we visualize the colors of the known spectrum and begin to identify and sense the inherent energy frequency that shows itself in the form of color and light, always remembering that the visual color seen is not the energy but the form the energy uses to express itself.

And so we come to the point of beginning to apply higher energy in a scientific way in the first step of purification.

In the analysis of thought-forms retained in the electro-magnetic field of a student, it is well to note that the creation of such forms follows the basic rule-a higher impulse acts upon a lower (energy-matter) substance and produces an intermediate form or consciousness. The retained thought-forms, common to all, are kept because the creative impulse was not strong enough to project them outside the aura or electro-magnetic field to accomplish a visualized purpose, and the created form remained attached to the creator to be a continuing influence. Thought-forms consist, therefore, of an impulsing energy holding matter-substance into a specific form however imperfect. Thought-forms vary in quality according to the high or low impulse which acts on matter either of high or low quality.

The aggregate of thought-forms above the head consist of true ideas precipitated into the lower mental planes as ideals suited to the development and environment of the creator. Customs, codes, conventions, rules of conduct, commandments, idols, angels and Gods, high motivations of all kinds find their representation here and remain even when outgrown and replaced by later development. They stand between the personal self and the true ideas needed for further spiritual growth and must eventually be eliminated.

As we move downward through the four zones already described in our consideration of these accumulations, we find thought-forms of increasing density and relating to the emotional nature, the instinctual nature and to the physical body itself in which case accumulations around the legs and feet actually inhibit movement in ways which affect the body itself as the body ages.

INVOCATION OF THE SOUL

We have spoken earlier of the statement in the BHAGAVAD-GITA in which the Soul says: "I put down a portion of myself but remain. . ." This "portion" appears as an almost invisible spark, usually covered by an iridescent cluster of forms which we have called "idealized thought-forms". In aspirants the spark is enlarged but still a small, pale globe of light. In those who have taken the first steps on the Path, it is bright and radiating somewhat. In Initiates of the Threshold the light above the head, the spark or soul-star becomes much larger and more radiant; when activated the brilliant radiance of the soul-star may extend several feet. This star is the physical (etheric) symbol of that portion of the soul "put down" into matter. It is linked with the soul, first by a thread and then by a band of expanding rainbow fire as fusion of personality and soul proceeds. This thread and, later, band is the etheric-astral-mental portion of the antahkarana or bridge which exists until final fusion of personality and soul takes place. This soul-star is the instrument or extension through which the soul works and ultimately changes the physical body through a definite, scientific process into a suitable vehicle through which it can function.

The personality may invoke and cooperate, but the soul-star is always the extension of Soul and will not respond to personality demands or experiments except for those that further its own purpose. The soul-star will not be expanded, exploded, whirled, projected or put through any personality gymnastics, and such efforts may interfere with its real function. Accordingly, the first approach of the personal self is to INVOKE THE SOUL.

The prime necessity for any student in the effort to learn how "to recognize, tap, channel and direct" spiritual energy is to enlist the cooperation of his own soul in the project. There is one certain way to achieve this; it involves the use of a very ancient mantram which has been used by students for thousands of years. The mind should be centered or concentrated in the soul-star located at a point about six inches above the head with the intent of soul cooperation with the aspiring personality held firmly in mind, and the words spoken *aloud* with a pause at the end of each line of the mantram. Each of these statements of affirmation produce certain results in the subtle bodies which will become evident to students as time passes; the significant one at the present stage will be noted in an increase in size, brilliance, and the radiation of the soul-star. This result indicates the eagerness of the soul to cooperate with the personality and the willingness to begin the infusion with higher types of energy and life. This mantram should become so much a part of the inner life that it is held constantly in the consciousness: *no work should be undertaken until this mantram has been said.* The words are as follows:

> I am the soul.
> I am the light divine.
> I am love.
> I am will.
> I am fixed design.

After the invocation or soul mantram, the soul-star will obey thought and move within the vehicles and immediate electro-magnetic field. It will expand or contract or send out a beam of energy without personality direction. It will also differentiate its white radiance into energies, some of which have familiar colors. These are only beginning powers of the soul-star. It is a most powerful, versatile and useful instrument of White Magic. *It will not respond for anything else!* In the process of building the Central Channel, the soul-star literally burns its way through hindering thought-forms and complexes to open a channel for the flow of higher energies. This produces debris or undesirable and no longer useful substance which must be cleared from the vehicles and fields. This clearing process is described a little later under the heading, The Spiritual Whirlwind.

Students generally understand the statements in the Soul Mantram except for the last one. The "fixed design" refers to the plan of the soul for the current incarnation. Within this plan, a person has freedom of choice and may live his life any way he wishes. If he makes mistakes, as all evolving people do, he will learn from them; if he follows the plan of the soul, he will evolve more rapidly and reap the benefits of his incarnation.

This ancient soul mantram, given by the Tibetan Master, Dwal Khul, in the book DISCIPLESHIP IN THE NEW AGE, Volume 2, is the first meditation outlined and it is the absolute beginning of *all* occult techniques. Without it or some form of it, nothing happens! No yoga practices, meditations, chantings, postures, breathings, etc. are effective. We have witnessed the failure of years of such practices which made *no change* in the inner vehicles of the aspirant. We have also witnessed that its use and presence in the brooding consciousness has made simple techniques rapidly effective in clearing and energizing the inner vehicles and in building radiant magnetic fields around purified forms. This is not to say that the dedicated and sincere work done by aspiring students has no effect whatever; it does test their dedication, persistence, and aspiration, and it is true that all "honest" work produces a just reward. But, with the use of the Soul Mantram, the aspirant activates the soul-star which expands and intensifies its radiation. In the course of time the remaining lines have the following effects:

I am the light divine.
The Central Channel flashes forth and intensifies. It becomes full of rainbow fire.

I am love.
A rose-pink downpour of energy from the heart of the soul-star floods the Central Channel.

I am will.
A royal purple, brilliant clear red, a white, or an indigo blue downpour enters and fills the Central Channel. Sometimes all of these energies are present or follow each other in sequence, and the order or sequence may vary. In time, three more subrays appear.

I am fixed design.
The sensitive points along the Central Channel flash forth with intense radiation; these later are the points occupied by the psychic centers or chakras. The fixed design is the plan of the soul for the current incarnation and is indicated by the energy components in the vehicles and their relative strengths.

The above descriptions of what occurs as the Soul Mantram is voiced are just the first noticeable reactions. Effects increase with time, application and progressive purification. As alignment with the Soul becomes more accurate and stronger and as personality integration develops, the ability of the lower bodies - mental, emotional, and etheric-physical - to respond together *as a unity* becomes definite and other results are obtained.

We have said that the basic thought-form (Plate 4) is built on a spiritual reality. The soul-star and a tiny thread extending from it down through the body are present realities. The soul-star is activated by the invocation and techniques given. The Central Channel is built to useful size by process and technique outlined in the first part of Phase 1 instructions to follow. The substitute centers or sensitive points along the Central Channel are constructed by the creative imagination. It is perhaps unfortunate at this stage that they have been given names and locations with reference to the physical vehicle; however, if it is *clearly understood* that the substitute centers are the product of the creative imagination, no harm will be done and the names and locations will have future value.

The invocation of the soul is described in INITIATION HUMAN AND SOLAR as Rule 2: " . . .application in triple form . . ." The rules in INITIATION HUMAN AND SOLAR are for applicants (aspirants, we have called them). In THE RAYS AND THE INITIATIONS, written years later, the same rules were given in a different form for initiates. Both should be read for *requirements have not changed.* Those students who have radiating soul-stars *are* First Degree Initiates, and it is assumed (let

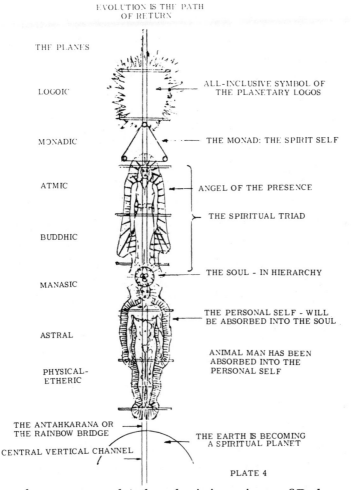

EVOLUTION IS THE PATH
OF RETURN

THE PLANES

LOGOIC — ALL-INCLUSIVE SYMBOL OF THE PLANETARY LOGOS

MONADIC — THE MONAD: THE SPIRIT SELF

ATMIC — ANGEL OF THE PRESENCE

THE SPIRITUAL TRIAD

BUDDHIC

MANASIC — THE SOUL - IN HIERARCHY

THE PERSONAL SELF - WILL BE ABSORBED INTO THE SOUL

ASTRAL

ANIMAL MAN HAS BEEN ABSORBED INTO THE PERSONAL SELF

PHYSICAL-ETHERIC

THE ANTAHKARANA OR THE RAINBOW BRIDGE

CENTRAL VERTICAL CHANNEL

THE EARTH IS BECOMING A SPIRITUAL PLANET

PLATE 4

us hope, correctly) that the injunctions of Rules for Applicants have been *lived* already to an effective extent, even though not fully demonstrated. Also *all* are ready for the effort to understand and make effective the rules for mature aspirants, initiates. The Tibetan Master has used words which indicate the "triple form", i.e., "deliberately stimulated, mentally appreciated, emotionally propelled". This is the rule for building and projecting a thought-form.

In the Soul Mantram the first line brings about identification with the soul as a manifested entity on the mental plane, the Solar Angel. The second, third and fourth lines are spoken *as if* the aspirant were the soul invoking its subjective being—manas buddhi, atma or higher mind, spiritual love and spiritual will. The fifth line states the plan or design of the soul for the personality for this incarnation, and its attitude, *as if*, indicates the cooperation and acquiescence of the personality to work with and to accept guidance from the soul which will and does then begin the work of building the inner light body. The inner light body built by the soul will ultimately infuse the purified and perfected personality so that the two will act and be as one, the soul-infused personality or the personality soul-infused. THE SOUL DOES THE WORK.

We call to your attention the initial fact of "enforced evolution": that spiritual beings came from Venus and undertook the age-long task of lifting mankind into the light. After forming the link with the animal men on Earth, they turned their attention to their own activities on their own level; these are group activities and involve use of what we term the higher principles or the spiritual triad of atma, buddhi and manas. In relation to human personalities, the soul is the true incarnator. It knows nothing of the lower planes except that which it contacts and retrieves through the lower bodies. Its manifestation on the lower levels is limited to that portion of itself which we call the soul-star through which we receive a minute part of Soul consciousness called Self-Consciousness.

After eons of time (not the same as our concepts of time) the personal soul vested in the soul-star awakens and turns its attention toward its source, its Father in Heaven, with aspiration; it begins to cooperate in Soul intent, and the Soul's response is instantaneous and joyous. The Soul's meditative attention becomes concentrated and rapid progress in Soul-personality integration can be consumated.

The ancient teaching impresses us with the need for the personal self *to act as if* it is the Soul *as far as possible* but to realize that the Soul's objectives are not those of the personal self and that its wisdom and power are far beyond the comprehension of the personal self. So the personal self is given the Soul Mantram: "I am the Soul . . .". We repeat—this mantram should become a central part of your consciousness and realization. Without this affirmation no technique of mind, emotional nature or physical action has any subjective result; such practices only stir the physical body, demonstrate persistence and strengthen aspiration. *The outer forms of the techniques we give are without result if not preceded by this Soul Mantram.*

It is the soul that does the work—that builds the Central Channel, sensitizes the points along the Channel to later receive the psychic centers, uses the Spiritual Whirlwind (later to be described), releases invoked energies to the aspiring student, raises the energies of substance and matter to blend with the invoked energies, builds the body of light, and ultimately absorbs the personal self which it no longer needs.

Cooperation of the personal self in the form of persistence, fiery aspiration, focussed attention while following the techniques is needed and required for success. It is as if the soul said, "I am here; be still and know and I will do all that is needed." But building the Central Channel is a cooperative effort between the soul and the personal self, even if not a great deal is required of the personality.

THE CENTRAL VERTICAL CHANNEL

We have spoken of the "thread" which is the beginning of the bridge. There are successive additions to this central thread until five main strands are complete. These additions are described by Dwal Khul in EDUCATION IN THE NEW AGE, page 143, in THE RAYS AND THE INITIATIONS in the Chapter called "The Science of the Antahkarana, pages 441-501. There are also references to the "channel" in LETTERS ON OCCULT MEDITATION.

As a bridge in consciousness on the mental plane the antahkarana or Rainbow Bridge is described as a symbolic triangle. The first link is made between the personality as an energy center called the Mental Unit and between the Soul focussed in the Causal Body or Egoic Lotus. It is this which is vitalized by the affirmation, "I am the Soul . . ." The successive statements relate to the Spiritual Triad focussed on the highest mental level, and the final statement relates to the link between the higher or abstract mind and the personal self focussed in the lower or concrete mind—the Mental Unit. Changes in the Central Vertical Channel show the completion of these linkages and the growth in spiritual attainment.

Plate 5 is based on the diagram on page 525 in the book, THE RAYS AND THE INITIATIONS, but contains more descriptive and definitive statements as explanation. The Initiations represent degrees of developed sensitivity and realized responsibility as spiritual progress is made. The Path of Return is the path of evolution from individual to group consciousness, and the difference between these two states of awareness and capacity are as great as the difference between animal and individual human consciousness. A detailed description of these differences in consciousness is given at the end of the book, DISCIPLESHIP IN THE NEW AGE, Volume 1.

That the antahkarana is described as a triangle of energy should not confuse the student, or that it is described as a bridge in consciousness on the mental plane. The reason for these variations in description is that space and time

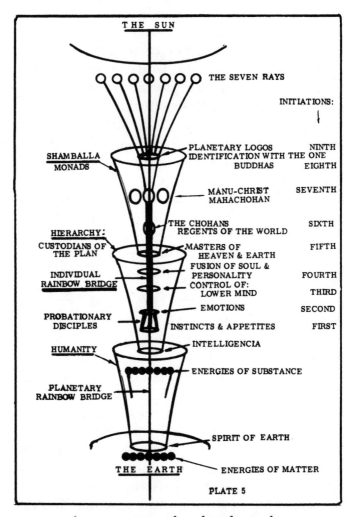

THE SUN

THE SEVEN RAYS

INITIATIONS:

SHAMBALLA
MONADS

PLANETARY LOGOS   NINTH
IDENTIFICATION WITH THE ONE
BUDDHAS   EIGHTH

MANU-CHRIST   SEVENTH
MAHACHOHAN

HIERARCHY:

THE CHOHANS   SIXTH
REGENTS OF THE WORLD

CUSTODIANS OF
THE PLAN

MASTERS OF   FIFTH
HEAVEN & EARTH

INDIVIDUAL
RAINBOW BRIDGE

FUSION OF SOUL &
PERSONALITY   FOURTH

CONTROL OF:
LOWER MIND   THIRD

EMOTIONS   SECOND

PROBATIONARY
DISCIPLES

INSTINCTS & APPETITES   FIRST

HUMANITY

INTELLIGENCIA

ENERGIES OF SUBSTANCE

PLANETARY
RAINBOW BRIDGE

SPIRIT OF EARTH

THE EARTH   ENERGIES OF MATTER

PLATE 5

are not the same on other levels as they are on the physical plane, and the effort to find correct analogies and descriptive words sometimes appear paradoxical or misleading. Objectively to clairvoyant vision, the antahkarana is manifested in the Central Vertical Channel and its condition and use and development is revealed there.

Although the activation and expansion of the Central Channel is necessary for the individual clearing processes, its most important aspect is its linking between the Planetary Logos and His physical vehicle, the Earth, as well as its importance as a transmitter of His energies through ourselves as units of intelligence within His Body.

The most important construction job anyone will ever undertake is to build a Central Channel through his energy structures through which His spiritual energies can flow and begin their redemptive work. This channel has been called by various names by different teachers and systems - the rod or staff, the middle pillar, the axis, the rainbow bridge, the antahkarana. Ultimately this channel forms the link between highest spirit and lowest matter.

The technique used to build the Central Channel is called *triangulation* because it consists of building mentally and imaginatively a series of small triangles, one side of which, when aligned, forms the vertical channel. It is an occult truism to say that "energy follows thought" and yet this is a literal and very important fact. As we direct our thought to the soul-star and invoke its response through the mind and mental processes of imagination and visualization, it is possible for us to direct the movement of the star with its soul energy in a controlled manner. By this mental direction of energy, a student is enabled to clear away a channel for the continuous flow of spiritual energies through the lower vehicles or bodies. This is a slow and gradual process because it must be done under control and without haste or carelessness. The points along the Central Channel used in the formation of the triangles are *not* the major psychic centers; they are sub-stitutes for the major centers at this stage. The real energy centers are outside the body due to the "loaded" condition of the vehicles. Later, when the channel becomes clear and straight, full of spiritual light and quite large, and the external thought-forms have been removed, the major centers will move into position at intervals where they belong along the channel.

It is suggested that, in the beginning, only the first triangle be formed during the prac-tice session for at least two weeks, omitting the "top of the head" which is within the soul-star's radiation. In the third week two more points - the throat and heart - may be added. The fourth week add the solar plexus; the fifth week add the sacral plexus; the sixth week add the base of the spine. Each week hereafter add one or two of the minor points until all triangles have been made and the Central Channel is completely through the vehicles. Always move the soul-star very slowly and deliberately in its upward motion. As in any container the heavier material in the body sinks to the bottom and requires more effort to remove it. When start-ing on the minor points or substitute centers, do the upper points more quickly and spend more time on the lower ones in order to bring the Central Channel into an even and equal development all the way through. There must be no blockage or tapering off of the channel; if there is, there may be a dispersion of energy at that point and consequently unpleasant and unfavorable effects. It is better to practice this technique too long and too much than to neglect any part of it!

The exact technique used to build the Central Channel is as follows:

1. Repeat the Soul Mantram, aloud if possible.

2. Concentrate your attention in the soul-star six inches above your head. If you cannot see it or sense it, visualize or imagine it as a small, brilliant sun. You will recognize its presence in time.

3. Mentally move the soul-star diagonally forward to a position just in front of the eyes, straight into the center of the head, and *slowly* straight upward to rest position six inches above the head.

4. Repeat Step 2 and 3 as you make the successive triangles at each sensitive point in the sequence given in the Diagram.

Those who have some knowledge in the kaleidoscopic field of occult investigation may take note and question what is obvious in our diagrams and descriptions, namely, that the Central Channel, the bridge, continues beyond vision *into the earth* as well as upward (the tradi-

TRIANGULATION
Substitute Centers or Sensitive Points

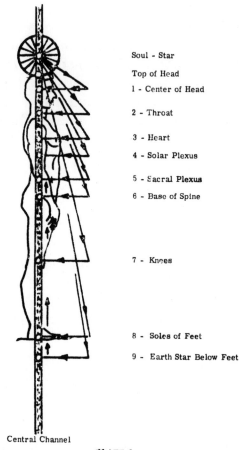

Soul - Star

Top of Head

1 - Center of Head

2 - Throat

3 - Heart

4 - Solar Plexus

5 - Sacral Plexus

6 - Base of Spine

7 - Knees

8 - Soles of Feet

9 - Earth Star Below Feet

Central Channel

PLATE 6

tional direction of Heaven). This linkage to earth was apparently deliberately omitted by Dwal Khul, probably for the reason that in the past efforts of many magicians (both developed and amateur) have focussed on the earth energies—energies of matter: earth, water, air and fire. These earth energies are the precipitating energies of materialization, and in their connection with the devic or angelic forces (the builders of form), they must be used for that last and most difficult step in evocation or descent into form. The higher correspondences of these energies were generally omitted by magicians or only implied with the result in some cases of unspeakable perversions and ceremonies ranging from the ridiculous to the most vicious and destructive. Such usage creates very bad karma for these practitioners.

In EXTERNALIZATION OF THE HIERARCHY, page 689, Dwal Khul says, " . . .the Hierarchy need not be further handicapped by working in substance while the forces of evil work both in substance and matter." This prophecy has been implemented and the recognition that man is a child of Earth as well as of Heaven is a necessary part of occult teaching, and Hierarchy *is* working also in matter *now*. Earth as the body of the Planetary Logos will be purified as the process of externalization continues. This necessity is common knowledge among the intelligencia and is now beginning to be recognized by mass consciousness, which is reacting to the suffering produced by wide-spread physical contaminations.

THE SPIRITUAL WHIRLWIND
OR ETHERIC VORTEX

The clouded condition of the electro-magnetic field or aura around the vehicles - mental, emotional or astral, and etheric-physical - of all persons, without exception, has been described in the foregoing pages and plates. The Tibetan Master, Dwal Khul, has spoken of this condition as consisting of "fogs and miasmas". Its accumulation is from two main sources:

1. Our contact with the fields of others, both individual, collective and planetary.

2. The product of the destruction of more resistant thought-forms in building, burning through, for the Central Channel and later from the disintegration of the more resistant thought-forms that adhere to the bodies.

This is a constant burden and menace to all and must be disposed of continually. There comes a time when the Causal Field or soul body becomes organized and intense enough to burn most of this gathered debris on contact. However, for a long time and always useful, there is an instrument of the Soul called the Spiritual Whirlwind or Etheric Vortex to use.

This Spiritual Whirlwind or Etheric Vortex is built of energy-substance of the highest etheric subplanes of the etheric physical, emotional and lower mental planes and is generally white in color which is the seventh (highest) atomic subplane. It is a spiritual reality, and we invoke it AS IF we were the Soul with the creative imagination "deliberately stimulated, mentally appreciated and emotionally propelled". This last step in Phase 1 is to remove the substance loosened and remaining in the field after the triangulation process is completed for the day (including two points, a few points, or all points on the Central Channel). Dwal Khul has said much about this vortex which He calls "the funnel". Its elementary use is to clear away the loose debris in the field, but it has a great many more uses also. (See LETTERS ON OCCULT MEDITATION, pages 191 to 296.)

To explain the vortex and how it works, it is necessary to use an analogy. It has been found in nature that air or water moving downward under the law of gravity (attraction) forms a vortex, whirlpool or cyclone. The direction or rotation is determined by location on the planetary surface, being reversed in the northern (clockwise) and southern (counter-clockwise) hemispheres. Three forces enter into the formation of a tornado: gravity, centrifugal force (outward-dispersion) and centripetal (inward - attractive) force. With these three in approximate balance, the form is maintained. A vacuum forms at the empty center. Heavier objects are carried into the vortex by currents of air moving to fill the vacuum at the center and are rotated in the rim, thrown off, or drawn down into the center.

Analogous principles and applications can be used to explain the vortex which is a rotating whirl of etheric energy. The vortex is started by focussing the mind in visualization far above the head outside the causal field (See Plate 7) which causes a downward rush of higher and more rarified energy-substance into lower and denser energy-substance. This energy is invoked by personality unification with the soul, by visualization of the vortex by the student and projection by the Soul. The tip or lowest point of the vortex follows the Central Channel (or the tiny thread, like a strand of spider web, which exists in everyone), and it moves downward, picking up the heavier substance (debris) not locked to the vehicles in thought-forms, that which has been released by their destruction in later techniques of redemption and purification, or any loose and drifting substance picked up from the environment and daily contacts. The vortex picks up and removes these unwanted and no longer needed substances and carries them deep into the earth where they are used to benefit the lower kingdoms evolving with humanity on the planet. All forms are constantly processing energy-substance: receiving, assimilating, eliminating. The spiritual vortex accelerates part of this system in a kind of spiritual ecology.

The size of the vortex and the frequencies (colors) used as well as the direction (from Left-to-Right in the Northern Hemisphere) are determined by the soul which sometimes takes over from the visualized program with a program of its own. This need not be of concern to students if, indeed, such control is recognized. As it gains strength and power, it follows the cycle of clearing without constant personal direction after the soul and the vortex have been invoked. The size, speed, nature of the energy used is all controlled by the soul and does not require personal direction and guidance. The vortex must not be interfered with

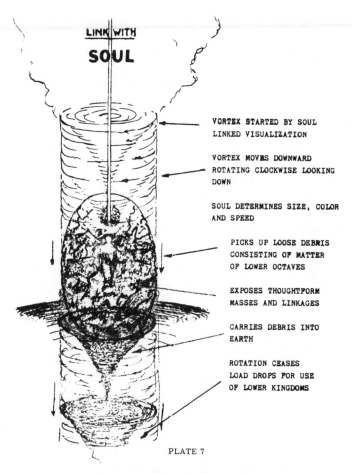

LINK WITH
SOUL

VORTEX STARTED BY SOUL
LINKED VISUALIZATION

VORTEX MOVES DOWNWARD
ROTATING CLOCKWISE LOOKING
DOWN

SOUL DETERMINES SIZE, COLOR
AND SPEED

PICKS UP LOOSE DEBRIS
CONSISTING OF MATTER
OF LOWER OCTAVES

EXPOSES THOUGHTFORM
MASSES AND LINKAGES

CARRIES DEBRIS INTO
EARTH

ROTATION CEASES
LOAD DROPS FOR USE
OF LOWER KINGDOMS

PLATE 7

by over-zealous aspirants but allowed to pass completely through and outside the causal field where, with its load of debris, it disappears in a zone or layer of the etheric body of the planet which we call the etheric fire or "burning ground". (This term has other more subjective occult applications.) The Whirlwind *does not* then hover around, move forward, and up again to the point where it entered the field upon invocation. When it drops its load which it carries out of the field and into the earth, it simply ceases to move and disappears. A "new" whirlwind must be invoked; and it is possible to invoke a whole series of whirlwinds to move through the vehicles and fields, giving the appearance of a column of light or soul fire moving through to the "burning ground". The whirlwind is not a *thing* although it has been called a "tool of the Soul".

The process of clearing the vehicles and field of loose debris, silt, and objectionable substance works rapidly but still takes measurable time, and the *process* must be repeated until such stuff is gone. This is an *elimination process* which is a basic part of the clearing technique, and it must be used constantly throughout the purification of the vehicles. The whirlwind will not dislodge the denser thought-forms or cage; another technique must be used in connection with the whirlwind and the next technique, Phase 2, describes the beginning of it. The technique of Phase 2 is not given in this book because it is best done with teachers or groups who can give the protection required, although individuals can do it successfully. This, as the Brothers have said, relates more to personal progress and is not needed by Hierarchy at this time as much as is the linking process made definite and useful by the Phase 1 processes.

As we said, when attention is turned away from the vortex and its movement deep within the earth, it stops rotating, drops its load and ceases to exist. Plate 7 shows the steps in this process which, when carried on consistently, clears the vehicles and their radiating magnetic fields of loose and contaminating debris, internal smog, which is constantly drawn toward and into the vehicles until radiating powers are attained to offset the effects of heavy fields and inner smogs of humanity.

It should be noted that this process of clearing with the whirlwind, at this stage of the work, should be continued for from three to five minutes. It is always better to use this practical and useful tool, the vortex, longer than is required. It should be used not only during and after the daily work (upon completion of the technique of Phase 1) but frequently during the day.

The question will occur to students: how can the aspirant know when the process is needed and when it is complete? To recognize this is a part of the training in sensitivity, the beginning of etheric, emotional and mental sense perception. Some aspirants "see" and "feel" or "sense" immediately. All arrive at a point very soon when the condition of the field shows to inner vision that they have somehow sensed when they are not clear. The development and nature of perception depends to a large extent upon the Ray or energy composition of the individual.

CHAPTER 6
GROUP FORMATION

The most important part of what has been written is the material in Chapter 5 which could be summed up thus:

1. Invocation of the Soul-star and its response

2. Use of the Soul Mantram

3. Building the Central Channel by the technique of triangulation

4. Use of the Spiritual Whirlwind. If this is done, and it can be completed effectively in from one to three months if a student really applies himself to the technique, the student will have become a channel for those energies so desperately needed in the world today.

In our wide observation of yogis, teachers

and students over many years, we have rarely
seen anyone with the Central Channel fully
developed. This applies to many true and dedicated workers. These sincere people generally
show an activated or radiant Soul-star, some
clearing in the upper part of the field around
the head, and the Central Channel built to the
throat. In one student, a Zen initiate, the Central Channel had been extended to the solar
plexus with only a thread beyond. This was a
dangerous condition and had caused decades
of suffering, for whatever it may mean to the
Soul, the physical body is not equipped to handle the spiritual energies which will go as far as
they can and then disperse. The Channel must
be completed into the earth to function properly and without unfavorable effects on the
physical body. Dispersion of the spiritual energies midway down the torso produced all kinds
of physical disease in that area because of too
rapid clearing and energy congestion. In DIS-
CIPLESHIP IN THE NEW AGE, Volume 2,
page 57, Dwal Khul speaks of release of "something from that which lies above to that which
lies below." On page 61 in the same book He
says "aspirants must be stable enough to stand
steady under the impact of hitherto undis-
cerned spiritual energy." Again on page 71 He
says, "The energies of dispersion are sudden
death to the physical vehicle if unprepared."
Consequently, we say the work must be *graded,
guarded and guided.* This applies more to the following phases of our teaching than to Phase
One. Since the Brothers have recommended

the release of the techniques of the First Phase, our opinion as to its safety has been confirmed. The emotional body of many aspiring students is on the Sixth Ray which has fanaticism in its negative aspect; this causes a vain self-assurance in these aspirants who are so dominated and often leads them into trouble. And so we advise caution in trying to force matters by using the more advanced meditations given in DISCIPLESHIP IN THE NEW AGE, Volume 2.

The Soul Mantram we use will be found on page 123, and there is much of great value in the text of this chapter. WE HAVE FOUND THAT, WITHOUT GUIDANCE, IT IS NOT ADVISABLE TO USE THE TECHNIQUE *IN FULL* UNTIL THE CENTRAL CHANNEL IS BUILT AND THE VEHICLES PURIFIED. It may be that the crisis of the present demands releases which will result in casualties like those in any battle. Accordingly, we warn disciples to proceed cautiously and according to directions. We can assure those who undertake the work as given that they will be observed when they become of service; and, as the old platitude says, "When the pupil is ready, the teacher appears." There is no objection to reading and studying the text of DISCIPLESHIP IN THE NEW AGE, Volume 1 and 2, and the other books of Alice A. Bailey through whom Dwal Khul gave us the teaching. On the contrary, it is the best preparation a student can make and it is emphatically advised that the books be read and studied.

GROUNDING ENERGY

It may be asked: "After building the Central Channel how shall I proceed?" WHEN THE CHANNEL IS BUILT, THE SOUL PROCEEDS TO USE IT FOR MANY FUNCTIONS WITH WHICH THE ASPIRANT NEED NOT BE CONCERNED AT FIRST. The whole aim of this book implies that those who are able (and we try to select them) will pass on what they have learned and assist those who come to them. This involves the beginnings of group activity and consciousness, and hopefully, when at least nine are working together, GROUP INTEGRATION. This last victory refers to a conscious union of the higher principles and may not be recognized by many whose higher principles are so involved. This was a principle goal for those to whom Dwal Khul addressed the letters and text of the two volumes of DISCIPLESHIP IN THE NEW AGE. It was *not* successful then as he stated, but since that time, changes in humanity and the influx of new energies has made it possible and enabled us to accomplish such an integration in our group (now called by the Brothers the Prototype Group).

Since what we propose is grouping, beginning with one or two and leading finally to conscious group cooperation, we add here what we have called and used for years: The Basic Group Meditation.

THE BASIC GROUP MEDITATION

We have been told that many energies can only be contacted and used in group formation. There are several things which can be inferred from this statement:

1. That there might be dangers in an attempt to use them individually and alone

2. That they might relate only to group activity, attitude and purpose

3. That they are of high order and require united strength, action and devotion to invoke

4. That no single individual can provide the balance of Ray energies required.

Before considering these suggestions in more detail let us consider why it is possible to work collectively at all. This possibility is the *basic inference*. Like man himself, the planet has an etheric body, and, as with man, this body projects slightly beyond the physical. If properly aligned and in proportion to size, the planetary etheric body would extend many miles, possibly forty miles, above the solid earth surface. In this we live and move and have our being. In this there is continuity of substance (matter-energy of a more subtle nature but still substantial). In this lies the possibility of telepathic interplay and communication and etheric linking generally. In this way we are never far apart or separate.

The human etheric body is built or woven of energy strands or threads, and correspondingly so is the planetary etheric body. Such analogies exist in every department of life and call attention to the *Law of Correspondence* which must always be used in connection with occult understanding. As with the human etheric body the strands of energy composing the planetary etheric body are concentrated in certain areas which are the etheric centers of the planet. Between these are stronger bands of energy and the sum total of these constitute the *planetary etheric network* to which we refer and into which we channel energies. We are thus, consciously or unconsciously, a part of the planetary etheric body, and our individual well-being and clearing is a contribution to planetary purification. There is also a vertical linkage symbolized and implemented by the Central Vertical Channel, and the sum total of these individual linkages constitutes the planetary vertical linkage called the Rainbow Bridge or the Planetary Antahkarana. Each incarnated Soul has a thread of this bridge, of this spiritual energy-substance, tiny and invisible except to the highest inner vision. When it is expanded by meditation and the techniques of clearing, it becomes a permanent channel filled with a continual downpour of a shimmering rainbow-like energy, and it is of immeasurable service to humanity and to Hierarchy. This is the vertical arm of the Fixed Cross; the horizontal arm provides for the distribution of energy into the planetary network.

Any group meditation is an augmentation, increase, or stimulation of this dual reception and transmission of energy by the intention, attitude and action of the disciples involved. The technique is simple, but its effectiveness requires certain development within disciples —the establishment of a Central Channel of measurable size, and a constantly increasing freedom from accumulated thought-forms in the vehicles and fields.

The diagram of the symbols of group relationships show the result of increasing numbers and potency. It should be observed that as the number of participants grows a network or field of energy or light is built. Also note that there is space at the center of the odd-numbered groups and a point in the center of even-numbered groups, and that as the numbers increase the space gets smaller and approaches a point.

There is a law of nature that whenever a form is built the ever-present undifferentiated life flows in and expresses itself according to the nature and capacity of the form. Thus we find at the center, a synthetic life-form which we call the group soul. The above statement, while fundamental, is over-simplified; that which flows in is of higher and more intense quality, being closer to the One Life but not identical with it. This is the Planetary Hierarchical Life

2   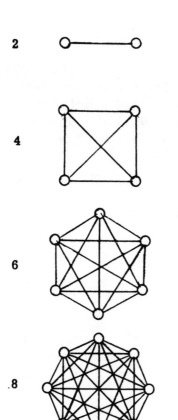   3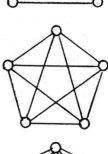

4   5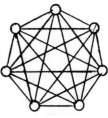

6   7

.8   9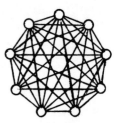

SYMBOLS OF RELATIONSHIP

PLATE 8

itself. This infusion is the goal of our group meditation and through it the group soul will become a permanent living entity; by the same rule and process we have defined as a part of the greater form, the planetary etheric body or its specialization, the Planetary Network, is developed and strengthened.

Now the planetary vehicles, like those of its individual human atoms, are clouded and covered with the "fogs and miasmas" precipitating in the physical vehicle today. There is a desperate need for "bringing in the light." This process, when carried on with increasing intensity and frequency, will make possible the externalization of the Hierarchy, the return of the Christ, and the inauguration of the Aquarian Age. We are told that the Hierarchy is experimenting with many groups. These groups may be identified by their common reference to and identification with the Soul—or with its inner manifestation—the Soul of the planet or the Planetary Hierarchy. Techniques and approaches, recognitions and terminology will vary, but the central identification will always be present.

We have been told also that a group of nine is the minimum number for channeling Hierarchical energies. Thus, when nine of our group were cleared of external thought-forms, a slow and painful but rewarding process, we established a permanent group network and invoked Hierarchical recognition. This was acknowledged by an intense downpour and consolidation of the group Soul. All of our group are members of the Planetary Hierarchy and have the power of *collective* invocation and *distribution.*

THE BASIC GROUP MEDITATION
Outline

1. *Group linking and integration.* In your creative imagination identify with your Soul-star and say the Soul Mantram: "I am the Soul. I am the Light Divine. I am Love. I am Will. I am Fixed Design." In a sweep of *attention* and *intention* around the group, known or unknown and seen or unseen, extend by your thought and intent a loving, unifying line of light to the Soul-star of each member of the group. The group Soul and network already exists; you need only to link into it.

2. Extend your line of light to the central light of the group Soul, the Master Dwal Khul or the Christ.

3. Say the Mantram of Unification:
   "The sons of men are one and I am one with them.
   I seek to love, not hate;
   I seek to serve and not exact due service;
   I seek to heal, not hurt.

   Let pain bring due reward of light and love,
   Let the soul control the outer form and life and all events,
   And bring to light the love which underlies the happenings
              of the time.

Let vision come and insight.
Let the future stand revealed.
Let inner union demonstrate and outer
cleavages be gone.
Let love prevail.
Let all men love."

These words, said with power and an understanding of their significance and with the potency of the mind and heart behind them, can
prove unbelievably potent in the life of the one
who says them. They will produce also an effect
in his environment, and the accumulated effects in the world will be great and effective. It
will change attitudes, enlighten the vision and
lead the aspirant to fuller service and to a wider
cooperation. This mantram is a modernized
and mystically worded version of the one which
was used widely in Atlantean days during the
period of the ancient conflict of which the present is an effect.

4. You have by this technique now linked and
   offered your personal contribution—*yourself.* The Guardians of the Network are now
   in control, and spiritual energies *may not be
   deflected* to lesser purposes and undeveloped and personalized aspirations.

5. Now you may say: "Identifying with the
   group, I direct the inflow of Hierarchical
   energies into the Planetary Network and
   help to implement their distribution by
   means of The Great Invocation:

"From the point of Light within the Mind of God
Let light stream forth into the minds of men.
Let Light descend on earth.

From the point of Love within the heart of God
Let love stream forth into the hearts of men—
May Christ return to earth.

From the center where the Will of God is known
Let purpose guide the little wills of men—
The purpose which the Masters know and serve.

From the center which we call the race of men
Let the Plan of Love and Light work out
And may it seal the door where evil dwells.

Let Light and Love and Power
Restore the Plan on Earth."

The Christ has said: "When two or three are gathered together in my name, there I shall be also." Obviously, He did not mean that he would be there in His physical, personal body or appearance, but rather that the energy of Love-Wisdom of which He, as head of the Planetary Hierarchy, is the highest expression, would be there. This, of course, includes the lesser forms such as our group soul, which receives and transmits such energies.

QUALIFIED PEOPLE

We have said a good deal about those who are qualified and can be successful with this technique. Hierarchical workers do not undertake impossibilities and discrimination in selecting students is important. For those who are clairvoyant, the condition of the Soul-star is very evident. If the Soul-star has some radiation, the person is probably a First Degree Initiate or close to it. Dwal Khul's books through Alice A. Bailey tell what this means in several places but chiefly in DISCIPLESHIP IN THE NEW AGE, Volume 1, at the end of the book and at various places well-outlined in THE RAYS AND THE INITIATIONS. We shall call attention from time to time to what He says in relation to techniques and the meaning of such attainment, for it *is* an attainment in spiritual growth and, in relation to the world population, rather rare but increasing rapidly as we have said. For those who cannot see or sense the Soul-star or the electro-magnetic field (the aura), questionnaires are helpful because they reflect insight, attitude, background knowledge, motive and a great many other subtle aspects of a person's growth. In the *Beacon Magazine* for May-June, 1971 a page appeared which was titled. "The New Consciousness: What is it?" We think these definitions may be helpful in determing who has "the new consciousness" and also helpful in developing a suitable questionnaire for screening applicants. The new consciousness demonstrates as:

Inclusiveness: reflecting a universality of outlook.

Relationship: knowing that all men are one in essence.

Balance: producing   clear   and   unbiased thought.

Realism: accepting facts and *things as they are.*

Initiative: Promoting change toward *what ought to be* through acceptance of personal responsibility.

Creativity: transcending   personal   ambition, the mind free to receive inspiration and perceive new ideas.

Love of truth: conceding that all truth is partial and relative, that there is no "absolute" or "only" truth, constantly expanding mental horizons can synthesize all facets of truth wherever found.

A sense of values: realizing that the values of the past are inadequate to the quality of human life to be evolved today. The   power   and   prestige   of possessions have no value in the light of today's material abundance.

A sense of social justice: realizing that the strug-
gle for freedom and equality is
the root cause of most social
problems in the world.

The "old fashioned virtues":   recognizing these as
the timeless, fundamental,
spiritual bases on which human
progress has eternally depended.
These include selflessness, love,
compassion, duty, generosity, in-
dustry or joy in work, trust and
trustworthiness, personal integ-
rity, dedication and commitment
to group good and the capacity
for steadfast, resolute action.

Essentially, therefore, the "new consciousness"
is a new dedication of the soul in man manifest-
ing its spiritual energy through the affairs of
daily life as responsibility and service.

—Taken from *The Beacon Magazine,*
May-June, 1971

Needless to say, we also expect those who undertake this work to have already developed
what is usually described as "character" with a
high standard of morality and ethical behavior.

A SCREENING QUESTIONNAIRE FOR SELECTION OF STUDENTS

We offer a possible questionnaire for selection of those who can profit from the technique
of building the Central Channel, but anyone
who decides to use this material with a group

should formulate his or her own questionnaire. Unfortunately not all First Degree Initiates are awake or inspired toward self-improvement. They vary widely, some being barely oriented to the work and responsibility for their Hierarchical status. We mention Dwal Kuhl's statement that "not much is required of them". Also there are many who have fanatical attitudes to cope with which leads them into all sorts of unwise activities and "unwise experiments". For our own group, the only requirements for admission in the beginning were (1) an active Soul-star, (2) a willingness to do the work *as given,* and (3) some financial contribution for necessary expenses. We assumed those who came to us to have aspiration, character, and moral and ethical standards.

It will not be a disaster if some who are not ready are given this opportunity. *The efficient use of time and energy prevents* us, as far as possible, from laboring with those who are uncertain, disobedient, uncooperative, and erratic in their application to the assigned work, always making excuses for not doing it and going off after will-o-the-wisps of the many cults and downright perversions of occult teaching. Even they will benefit, for no sincere effort is ever lost; such efforts teach what *not* to do and will enable students to have better discrimination next time. However, there are too many ready, responsive and eager students for us to waste time with the merely curious, those who think they know more than we do, or the unwise experimenters.

QUESTIONNAIRE FOR USE BY
STAR-GROUP TEACHERS

(Sample)

1. Are you concerned about the world and what is going on in countries other than your own?

2. Do you believe that all men are one in essence, that the human race is one kingdom evolving with other kingdoms on this planet?

3. Are you able to think clearly and without emotion coloring how and what you think? Are you biased and prejudiced? About what?

4. Can you face the facts in your life and in yourself or do you prefer to deny or ignore what is weak and wrong in yourself?

5. What responsibility do you have to yourself? your associates? your community? your country? the world? Which responsibility is the most important to you? Why?

6. Is your mind open to new ideas? or do you block off what is new by measuring it against what you already believe to be true?

7. Do you believe in reincarnation? Why or why not?

8. Can men ever be equal or free? When and how?

9. Should men have total opportunity according to their capacities? And material reward according to their productivity?

10 Truth has been guiding mankind from the beginning and such truths as men have perceived are as true as ever. The Aquarian Age will not repudiate that part of Truth revealed in the past. Do you believe this?

THE DIVINE WILL

It is known that the Planetary Logos (or God of this planet) is releasing the energy of the Divine Will directly to humanity, without the modification and stepping-down by Hierarchy, for the first time since humanity was individualized millions of years ago. This is an energy that comes from the Monadic level of consciousness and is described as POWER.

Response to this energy will come first from groups and will produce effects according to the nature of the group it impacts. Results will vary widely in both constructive and destructive directions as the *immediate* future will demonstrate. Individual response will be rare, for, as we have said, such energies are destructive to impure and undeveloped vehicles. Desire, which is a very low manifestation of will, will govern individual response in most cases.

We suggest that after a group, nine if possible, achieve some degree of outer integration, that the whole mantram on pages 123 and 141, in DISCIPLESHIP IN THE NEW AGE, Volume 2, be *used as a group.* The work on the centers should be omitted until much clearing and purification of the inner vehicles has been accomplished because work with the centers would not be effective without such inner purification and could cause serious emotional difficulty.

We are not available for casual interviews,

readings, interpretations, speaking engagements, etc. We can be reached through the publisher but do not guarantee a *physical* answer. If, as we believe (and know), there are those who have the vision to confirm what we have said to any extent clairvoyantly, we would like to contact them, for we have additional material from our own experience which may be valuable to them.

It is part of the program of externalization for the workers "in the vineyard" to contact each other and work together. This does not mean the type of publicity which money seekers use. Their highly publicized teachings are of little real value and in most cases are compilations from numerous sources—plagiarisms—to which credit is not given. So many today are trained researchers that such a result could easily have been predicted since moral and ethical judgment has not kept up with development in other skills.

This book is a beginning and will be followed by other writings if response justifies it.

CONCLUSION

In closing, we shall restate the purpose of this book:

1. To find those members of the New Age of Aquarius, the New Group of World Servers, who are qualified by evolutionary development to undertake certain successful techniques for spiritual development and planetary service in this period of crisis.

2. To present the First Phase of what we call clearing in The Science of Applied Energy.

3. To stimulate such aspirant-disciples to build the Central Vertical Channel which is the link between the Soul and the personality, to invoke the link between the Soul and the Spiritual Triad, and lastly to form the link between the Spiritual Triad

and the personal self.

We cannot overestimate the importance of this work and its value to the externalization forces of Hierarchy, for, without the cooperation of incarnated disciples, the Kingdom of Heaven cannot be brought to earth nor the Christ return to complete His work. Dwal Khul said on page 102 in DISCIPLESHIP IN THE NEW AGE, Volume 2: "One of the major recognitions which is essential to the spiritual aspirant is that the Hierarchy is completely unable- under the law of the freedom of the human soul- to work in the world of men without those representative groups which can 'step down' the hierarchical quality of energy so that the average man (with his average vibration and quality) can find in himself a point of response." And again on page 110 He says: "The coming cycle is momentous in its offering of opportunity, and I would have you - again as individuals and as a group - measure up to this chance. Fix your eyes on human need and your hand in mine (if I may speak thus to you in symbols) and go forward with me to greater influence and deeper usefulness."

The Central Channel is a magnetic tube or conductor through which a rainbow fire flows. Its magnetic surface insulates it from the bodies or vehicles, although radiation from it soon begins (after it becomes about one inch in diameter) and continues to increase as the Central Channel increases in size until the entire body is within the light of its radiation. Such a field aids the student, the Hierarchy and humanity greatly. Also in later processes of purification, transmutation and energizing it is invaluable.

Plates 4 and 5 are representative of the Central Vertical Channel, the Rainbow Bridge between Heaven and Earth.

The goal of externalization is not so much to enable individuals to reach a heavenly state of consciousness as it is to *bring it to earth:* it is not enough to think and meditate about this transformation. It is up to the aspirants and disciples of the world to make practical application of what they know through climbing the ladder of evolution in consciousness and to apply the principles of the Aquarian Age. In so doing, the young disciples will change all of the seven departments of human activity, civilization and culture into something which cannot be anticipated or visualized at the present time. The work proposed is to hasten the day - "to shorten the days without which no flesh shall live." *This will be a sufficient goal for those who respond.* May the increasing tensions of the changeover to the New Age of Aquarius be transmuted into right action, feeling and thought by the Children of the Dawn.

Two Disciples

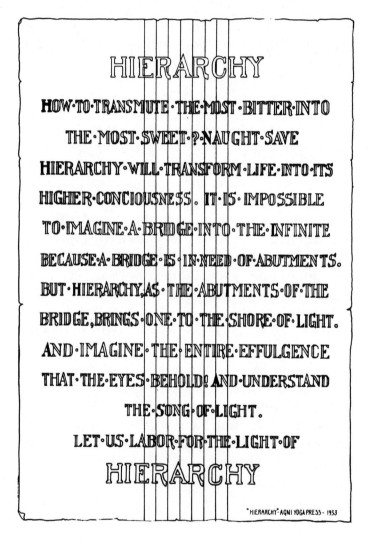

HIERARCHY

HOW·TO·TRANSMUTE·THE·MOST·BITTER·INTO
THE·MOST·SWEET·?·NAUGHT·SAVE
HIERARCHY·WILL·TRANSFORM·LIFE·INTO·ITS
HIGHER·CONCIOUSNESS.·IT·IS·IMPOSSIBLE
TO·IMAGINE·A·BRIDGE·INTO·THE·INFINITE
BECAUSE·A·BRIDGE·IS·IN·NEED·OF·ABUTMENTS.
BUT·HIERARCHY,AS·THE·ABUTMENTS·OF·THE
BRIDGE,BRINGS·ONE·TO·THE·SHORE·OF·LIGHT.
AND·IMAGINE·THE·ENTIRE·EFFULGENCE
THAT·THE·EYES·BEHOLD!·AND·UNDERSTAND
THE·SONG·OF·LIGHT.
LET·US·LABOR·FOR·THE·LIGHT·OF

HIERARCHY

"HIERARCHY"·AGNI YOGA PRESS - 1933

ADDENDA

Following the full moons of April, May and June in 1974 and at the annual Convocation of Hierarchy, the word came to the disciples of the world:

1. Do not fear when world conditions and their impact seem to produce hopelessness and despair for the underlying purpose is benign. Use if necessary the mantram on page 239 of WHITE MAGIC: "Let Reality govern my every thought and truth be the master of my life."

2. Learn to accept and transmit *spiritual will.* This is embodied in the words of the Christ, "Thy will be done!" Know, feel, and use this mantram of power. *The opportunity is great.* It is the sword, the spiritual will, which the Christ will bring when He walks among us. As disciples, it is ours to use "in the wisdom of the Soul."

3. Use the Soul Mantram. This statement is a part of Dwal Khul's first meditation as given in DISCIPLESHIP IN THE NEW AGE, Volume 2 and it is the heart of *all* successful techniques.

4. Build the Central Channel as instructed in this book.

5. Use the Spiritual Vortex, called "the funnel" by Dwal Khul or "the Whirlwind" in the BIBLE.

THE GREAT INVOCATION

FROM THE POINT OF LIGHT WITHIN THE MIND OF GOD
LET LIGHT STREAM FORTH INTO THE MINDS OF MEN.
LET LIGHT DESCEND ON EARTH.

FROM THE POINT OF LOVE WITHIN THE HEART OF GOD
LET LOVE STREAM FORTH INTO THE HEARTS OF MEN.
MAY CHRIST RETURN TO EARTH.

FROM THE CENTER WHERE THE WILL OF GOD IS KNOWN
LET PURPOSE GUIDE THE LITTLE WILLS OF MEN.
THE PURPOSE WHICH THE MASTER KNOWS AND SERVES.

FROM THE CENTER WHICH WE CALL THE RACE OF MEN
LET THE PLAN OF LOVE AND LIGHT WORK OUT
AND MAY IT SEAL THE DOOR WHERE EVIL DWELLS.

LET LIGHT AND LOVE AND POWER
RESTORE THE PLAN ON EARTH.

ANTAHKARANA

Publication and distribution of THE RAINBOW BRIDGE has been successful, that is, the book has reached many First Degree Initiates who are disciples of sufficient evolutionary development to recognize and undertake the work which relates to the First Rule in WHITE MAGIC, page 51, and COSMIC FIRE, page 997. And more importantly, groups have been formed to use the techniques given. Within the period of one year, since the first publication date, several thousand disciples have begun the work of invoking and blending the down pouring energies of Soul and Spirit with the evoked forces of substance and matter. The Synthesis of these energies pours directly into the Plan of Externalization of the Spiritual Hierarchy. Not all have seen or read the book, but all have contracted the thought form on the level of the concrete mind and are responding to its purpose by "modifying, qualifying and adapting" the idea as it seems best to them.

Since the publication of the first edition of this book two books containing additional information have been released. The first is Rainbow Bridge II. This book describes the Phase II techniques for clearing away hindering thought patterns, and is the next step after the application of the Phase I techniques. Rainbow Bridge II expands on the teachings in this book and includes the Phase I techniques as well. The second book, Rainbow Bridge Visualization, is a series of full page illustrations of the Phase I visualizations. A video tape with animation showing the same visualizations is in production at this time and will be available in early 1988.

All three books are available from: Rainbow Bridge Productions, P.O. Box 929, Danville, CA 94526.

Answers to questions about the techniques and further teachings, and information about groups or individuals doing Rainbow Bridge work in your area also may be obtained by writing to this address. Please send a check for $5.00 to help cover the costs of answering correspondence.

This plate, in color, is a part of Phase 2 instructions. It is inserted here to show what can be done in three to five years use of Phase 2 techniques. The electromagnetic field (the aura) has been cleared of all debris including both ancient and recently built thoughtforms; the Soul Star is very strong and the central channel (the antahkarana) is well defined. The health aura is not inhibited by adhering thoughforms. The astral and larger mental bodies are clear but unorganized. The centers are shown as minor centers, which is usual at this stage of evolution. The background is the casual field which is very large and is filled with various energies which have accumulated during the clearing processes as a reservoir of power. This disciple is ready to begin work on the obstructions and hindrances which fill the body itself and which require a different technique to eliminate.

The processes of clearing which are required formerly have been done in retreats or ashrams after the second initiation but, because of the Seventh Ray impact and the direct intervention of the First Ray by the Logos, it is possible to accomplish much clearing now as a part of the preparation of disciples to be workers in the processes of Externalization of the Hierarchy.

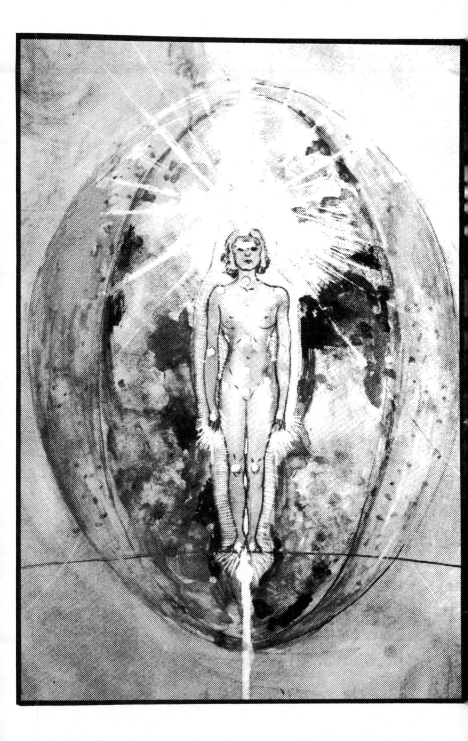

THE RAINCLOUD OF
KNOWABLE THINGS

"There is to be found today in the realm of intuition much of wonder; this can be contacted. It
is now the privilege of the race to contact that
'raincloud of knowable things' to which the ancient seer Patanjali refers in his fourth book; the
race through its many aspirants, can today
precipitate this 'raincloud' so that the brains of
men everywhere can register the contact. Hitherto this has been the privilege of the illumined and
rare seer. In this way the New Age will be
ushered in and the new knowledge will enter into
the minds of humanity.

"This can be practically demonstrated if those
who are interested . . . can attune themselves to
think clearly, and with a poised and illumined
mind seek to understand what is relatively a new
aspect of truth."

This wonderful privilege requires nothing but
an honest need for the truth. It is a gift to
humanity! The "Affirmation of the Disciple" on
page 191 of this book assists the disciple in gain-
ing the attitude that allows him to contact the
"Raincloud of Knowable Things". On page
196-7 of "Telepathy" by Alice A. Bailey is a
clear statement of what must be done: "The
disciple has to take himself as he is, at any time,
with any given equipment, and under any given
circumstances; he then proceeds to subordinate
himself, his affairs and his time to the need of the
hour — particularly during the phase of group,

national or world crisis. When he does this within his own consciousness and is, therefore, thinking along the lines of true values, he will discover that his own private affairs are taken care of, his capacities are increased and his limitations are forgotten.''

When the contact with the intuition is first made the impulse is to go deeper into the beautiful realms; if that is done, all you will remember is that you had a wonderful experience. If you stand on the threshold; ''And standing thus revolve, and tread this way the way of men, and know the way of God''; you will get the answer you want always.

The contact is most easily made by synchronously meditating groups, though do not think it is too difficult for individuals. It was reached by the author long before he was cleared of patterns, and before he knew not to ask foolish questions, which were answered just the same.

For more information on the ''Raincloud of Knowable Things'' see the following references to books by Alice A. Bailey:

Esoteric Psychology, Vol. I, p. 12
Telepathy and the Etheric Vehicle, p. 196-7
The Light of the Soul, pages 38, 424-5

Norman Stevens 11/87